The Hidden History of Co...

Coaching in Practice series

The aim of this series is to help coaching professionals gain a broader understanding of the challenges and issues they face in coaching, enabling them to make the leap from being a 'good enough' coach to an outstanding one. This series is an essential aid for both the novice coach eager to learn how to grow a coaching practice, and the more experienced coach looking for new knowledge and strategies. Combining theory with practice, the series provides a comprehensive guide to becoming successful in this rapidly expanding profession.

Published and forthcoming titles:

The Hidden History of Coaching

Leni Wildflower

Open University Press

Open University Press
McGraw-Hill Education
McGraw-Hill House
Shoppenhangers Road
Maidenhead
Berkshire
England
SL6 2QL

email: enquiries@openup.co.uk
world wide web: www.openup.co.uk

and Two Penn Plaza, New York, NY 10121-2289, USA

First published 2013

A catalogue record of this book is available from the British Library

ISBN-13: 978-0-33-524540-6 (pb)
ISBN-10: 0-33-524540-4 (pb)
eISBN: 978-0-33-524541-3

Library of Congress Cataloging-in-Publication Data
CIP data applied for

Typesetting and e-book compilations by
RefineCatch Limited, Bungay, Suffolk
Printed and bound by CPI Group (UK) Ltd, Croydon, CRO 4YY

Fictitious names of companies, products, people, characters and/or data that
may be used herein (in case studies or in examples) are not intended to
represent any real individual, company, product or event.

The **McGraw·Hill** Companies

"This book gives you the real story on who came before us and how we built on the learning to evolve coaching as an emerging profession. It's interesting, exciting, and a little bit scary to see some of the antics that brought us here. Yet the honesty and openness within this book and the commentary by the writer, demonstrates the values and beliefs we hold as coaches. It brings clarity to the past, and it strengthens the framework for what's possible as we continue forward."
Diane Brennan, MBA, MCC, Past President International Coach Federation (2008)

"Leni Wildflower's book provides an answer to the question 'What are the roots of coaching?' This answer contributes to addressing the follow-up questions 'What are the theoretical underpinnings of coaching?' and 'How can the underlying theories shape my practice as a coach?' If you are looking for the answer to any of these questions, read this book."
David Megginson, Emeritus Professor of HRD, Sheffield Business School, UK

"This book is unique. It offers readers both an inside perspective about the names who have made coaching and a critical analysis of the ideas, theories and concepts which have shaped coaching as the leading personal development strategy for the 21st century. Leni's clear writing style offers the reader a ring side seat for this journey through the history of coaching."
Professor Jonathan Passmore, Evora University

For Annette Baran
1927–2010
A wise and loving mentor and a precious friend

Table of contents

Series editor's preface

Over the years that I have trained many hundreds of new coaches, I am struck by how little they tend to know about the history of the craft they are learning. Many assume that it is a branch of management development or organization consulting. Others are vaguely aware that it might have something (though they hope maybe not too much) to do with therapy. Yet others wrongly attribute the whole thing to one or two of the people who came into coaching from a sports background. In fact I realize now that I was as confused and half-informed as any of my students.

This book is unique in tracking not just the tangled roots of what we now call coaching but also for in its insights into the people who were the founders or developers of so many of the movements, therapies and theories which have influenced us. Some of these people turn out to have been distinctly peculiar; others just intriguing in their ability to have been in the right place at the right time or to write about it compellingly. Some knew and influenced each other, especially those who floated into that giddily optimistic and eccentric community at Esalen in the early 1970s.

As coaches we need to know where our ideas and theories come from. When we are furnished with such knowledge we are in a much better position to understand where and when to call on one technique rather than another. We need to know that 'therapy' is not just a monolithic entity but can blend many different philosophies, some of which are deadly rivals and some of which have had a profound impact on coaching. We need to be able to distinguish one guru from another, including those whose promises have proved false. Knowing all of this will mean that we are also much better placed to answer challenges from clients who, today, are much more likely to ask us probing questions about which type of coaching we do as well as who and what has influenced our own practice. To reply lamely with the name of the school that trained you is no longer enough.

Leni Wildflower is an unusual voice in coaching. She combines many years of practice as a coach with the breadth of academically based thinking developed during her stint as innovator and Director of the Evidence-Based Coaching Programs at Fielding Graduate University in California. She has taught coaching all over the world and brings humour, insight and depth to everything she does. You will enjoy this readable book. It fills a serious gap in our understanding of the origins, development and practice of coaching.

Jenny Rogers
Series editor

Acknowledgements

It is not often that someone comes along who is a true friend and a good writer.

E. B. White: *Charlotte's Web*

This book would not have happened without the support, intelligence, encouragement and love of Joe Treasure, who took precious time away from his novel writing to help with this project.

Jenny Rogers believed in the book, twisted my arm to write it, and gave me constant, skilful and invaluable feedback – both personal and professional.

I owe a great deal to these two writers: my wonderful husband and my brilliant friend.

Foreword

How long has coaching been going on? As a defined procedure known by its own name? Twenty years, maybe. As a formalized activity, separate from therapy or training or conversation? Maybe 30 or 40 years. But – before all that – how long have people been engaging each other in the kind of conversation in which, if we overheard it, we'd catch a coaching flavour? It's almost impossible to know. Before people started making fly-on-the-wall documentaries, and pointing video cameras at each other, private conversations went almost entirely unrecorded. We depend on the occasional diarist for snippets of remembered dialogue. Were there particular wise and skilful teachers, mentors, priests, parents, friends, who held themselves back from persuading and instructing, who pushed aside their own needs, fears and desires for long enough to pursue a line of open questions, with no end in view except to create, in someone else, a space for reflection? It's inconceivable that there were not; that this never occurred.

Personally I grew up with questions with predetermined answers like 'Who made you?' (*God made me*) and 'What were the principle qualities of the American frontiersman?' (*The American frontiersman was tough, rugged, independent*). There were also rhetorical questions like 'What time do you call *this*?' and invitations to express an opinion on a defined topic: fox hunting: for or against? But 'What do you want?' unrelated to birthdays or school pudding, and asked without a trace of annoyance or exasperation – this question didn't feature. And as I moved into adulthood all the early decisions went largely unexamined, decisions that would shape the path of my life for years to come. The particular challenge and indulgence of being asked to account for myself – *to* myself – has been a later discovery.

But what about everyone else? What about the world's population stretching back over the centuries? In the absence of documentary footage, how could we ever know? Is there any literary evidence of a coaching style before the invention of coaching? A friend suggests Socrates, the great Athenian philosopher, whose dialogues were recorded by his student Plato. But Socrates is the master of the closed question, forever steering his students on relentless intellectual journeys:

> SOCRATES: Well, does anybody want to be unhappy and unfortunate?
>
> MENO: I suppose not.

SOCRATES: Then if not, nobody desires what is evil, for what else is unhappiness, but desiring evil things and getting them?

MENO: It looks as if you are right, Socrates . . .

Instead, I think of Horatio, Hamlet's only true friend in a court full of false ones. Horatio is a deeply sympathetic figure, even though his own story and his own concerns are largely absent from the play. Hamlet admires him for not being 'passion's slave'. He is a loyal friend, concerned for Hamlet's well-being, but with nothing to gain from him; an attentive listener who rarely expresses an opinion. When he does, finally, offer advice, it takes a very particular form. Hamlet has been challenged to a dual, a fight in which he will be villainously killed with a poisoned sword. Privately Hamlet confesses a sense of misgiving:

HAMLET: Thou wouldst not think how ill all's here about my heart.

HORATIO: If your mind dislike anything, obey it.

There you can hear the authentic coaching note: obey your own mind; trust yourself.

There's a conversation in Charles Dickens' novel, *Great Expectations*. Pip, the hero and narrator, is sitting by a river with his friend, an older girl called Biddy. Tearing at the grass, Pip tells her that he wants to be a gentleman because it's uncomfortable to be told that he's 'coarse and common'. Biddy asks him, 'Who told you so?'

'The beautiful young lady at Miss Haversham's, and she's more beautiful than anybody ever was, and I admire her dreadfully, and I want to be a gentleman on her account.' Having made this lunatic confession, I began to throw my torn-up grass into the river, as if I had some thoughts of following it.

'Do you want to be a gentleman to spite her, or to gain her over?' Biddy quietly asked me, after a pause.

'I don't know,' I moodily answered.

'Because, if it is to spite her,' Biddy pursued, 'I should think – but you know best – that might be better and more independently done by caring nothing for her words. And if it is to gain her over, I should think – but you know best – she is not worth gaining over.'

It's a nice moment. Biddy clearly knows what she thinks, but her attempt to lead Pip to think for himself by asking him a challenging question has something of that coaching flavour I'm looking for.

It isn't much; these are the best examples I can think of (the reader might do better). There are a lot of helpful friends in nineteenth-century novels, but they generally give advice or take out their cheque books.

Is it because a coaching conversation is inherently undramatic – because fiction demands conflict, a clash of agendas, raised passions on both sides? Perhaps. And yet it seems to me that you can hardly turn on the television at this point in the twenty-first century without catching some soap opera character, or the girlfriend of some troubled policeman, asking a question from a position of disinterested concern. In between 'Where were you on the night your wife was murdered?' and 'What the hell do you mean, you're seeing someone else?' we'll hear someone say 'Are you sure this is what you really want?' and 'What would you do right now if you could do anything?' and 'Meanwhile, who's taking care of *you*?'

I'm not saying good coaching has become commonplace. I'm sure it hasn't. But, in a general sense, the concept of the coaching conversation has entered our shared consciousness. The influence may not be direct. More likely it has gradually seeped into our awareness over a longer time from coaching's clinical ancestors, therapy and counselling; or it has come from the popularizations of humanistic psychology and transactional analysis, telling us that everyone has it in them to be OK, even to find joy, given half a chance; or it has reached us via countless self-help books offering the possibility that we can make more of ourselves.

It is this complex network of interweaving influences that is the stuff of this book. It contains amazing stories of individual brilliance, inspiration and courage; of muddle-headed pursuits and single-minded enterprises. There are particular hothouses of creative activity, such as Freud's Vienna and the Esalen Institute in 1960s California. Visionary figures like Carl Jung keep cropping up in other people's stories. The Nazis play an inadvertent role, encouraging gifted European Jews to find freedom and academic funding in American universities. There are plenty of heroes and a few hucksters, and, at every point, flashes of intellectual debate as one theorist or practitioner or popularizer builds on, or reacts against, the thoughts of another. Above all, this is the story of an idea: that we are not at the mercy of the material conditions of our lives and that there are, for most of us, untapped possibilities for experiencing life more richly and with greater happiness.

Joe Treasure

Introduction

For some years now I have been saying to my coach friends that without Carl Rogers and Werner Erhard coaching would not exist. I finally decided to challenge this somewhat glib assertion and the result is *The Hidden History of Coaching*.

I am part of what historians often refer to as the sixties generation. I began university in Vermont in the mid-1960s, but left in the middle of my second year to join an organization called Students for a Democratic Society. As a young woman, I was moved by the unfolding drama of the Civil Rights movement in the southern states. By 1965 I was living in poor neighbourhoods and working as a community organizer, which meant helping people to get welfare assistance, protesting against poor living conditions, and encouraging local residents to stand up to the landlords and abusive local police. Later I organized demonstrations against the war in Vietnam, ran an anti-Vietnam War coffee house, and was active in the emerging women's movement. I eventually returned to finish my education, but I learned much during my 'activist' years.

As the decade wore on I had an increasing desire to learn more about myself; to understand my feelings and motives. Most importantly, I wanted to feel happier, to find some inner peace. Political activism wasn't enough. I embarked on a period of psychotherapy, meditation, enlightenment intensives, and self-help seminars, including *est*. What I learned about myself was invaluable and frames a lot of what I instinctively do today as a coach. I'm still political, but I now blend political realities with psychological understanding. I believe it has made me a more whole, more compassionate human being.

This book is a series of stories – about politics and psychology and a lot more. As a history, it is selective and not always completely objective. It is certainly not an exhaustive survey of all the disciplines on which coaching is based. Instead, I have chosen an eclectic range of brilliant theoreticians, eccentric teachers, maverick therapists and inspirational movements that have contributed to our profession. Here are some of the stories I have included:

- The emergence, out of the darkness of the Great Depression, of Napoleon Hill, Dale Carnegie, Alcoholics Anonymous and the self-improvement movements of the early twentieth century.

- The founding of the Esalen Institute and stories of the many people who frequented this amazing place: Carl Rogers, Abraham Maslow, Virginia Satir, Aldous Huxley, Alan Watts, Will Schutz, Gregory Bateson and Sir John Whitmore, among others.
- The strange tale of Jack Rosenberg, who dropped out of his life to reinvent himself as Werner Erhard and take the self-help movement by the scruff of the neck.
- Fascinating personal glimpses of Sigmund Freud and Carl Jung, Erik Erikson and Eric Berne, Fritz Perls and Wilhelm Reich, and of how their lives shaped their thinking – and subsequently ours.
- The evolution of psychometrics – from the IQ number crunchers, to the celebration of human complexity.
- The impact on the individual of the social environment – from dark insights into obedience and groupthink, to what lies behind the soothing smiles of flight attendants.

Each chapter begins with a passage of reflection from a working coach, related to the content of the chapter, and ends with some implications for coaching. But the real richness is to be found in the stories. We all need stories to make sense of our lives. I hope these ones will give you food for thought – and a bit of inspiration too.

Coaching, like any creative human activity, has its exploiters eager to cash in, and its carping opponents, many of whom know our work only from the tabloids. But the popularity of coaching, its growth around the globe, and the way it has been embraced by hard-headed organizations prove that it answers a need. Coaching is remarkably diverse, but rests solidly on established principles. It has the capacity to make individual lives more fulfilled, but could also have a transformative impact on society. Given its profound origins and the richness of its hidden history, we should expect of it nothing less.

Leni Wildflower
July 2012

Part 1
Here comes everybody

Everyone has inside of him a piece of good news. The good news is that you don't know how great you can be! How much you can love! What you can accomplish! And what your potential is!

Anne Frank

Go confidently in the direction of your dreams. Live the life you have imagined.

Henry David Thoreau

Chapter 1: Self-help in hard times: the early motivational gurus

In my role as an executive coach, I know that my optimistic, positive attitude makes a significant difference for my clients. For me there is a big difference between optimism and simple positive thinking. Optimism is a sincere belief in the capacity to influence positive outcomes regardless of circumstances; positive thinking alone is 'wishful thinking' without commitment to take action. Time and time again, clients realize the power of optimism where I really believe in their goodness and potential. Optimism is infectious and helps clients to become more and more comfortable to practise being their 'best self'. And this starts a new habit and creates new self-awareness.

I have witnessed the power of optimism, positive visualization and BIG thinking. Positive attitude coupled with regular actions towards a desired state distinguishes dreamers from achievers. Without positive thinking we don't dare to dream big. And without consistent action, the goal remains in the thought-realm as a 'dream without legs'. This is the power of coaching with a positive frame of mind – facilitating clients to identify their core values and goals, to develop a positive attitude, to co-design actions towards their desired objectives, and to take time along the way to observe and celebrate what is shifting. I have witnessed profound growth in the client's capacity to move through strong emotions and handle unexpected events with ease and peace of mind. The magic of listening with a positive frame leaves an open space for clients to discover themselves in a world without judgement. Trust in my client and a positive, optimistic regard can be what is needed to create the shift and make the difference in my client's attitude and behaviour. In the words of Chinese philosopher Lao Tzu: 'At the centre of your being you have the answer; you know who you are and you know what you want.'

Virginia Williams, MBA, Professional Certified Coach ICF
Geneva, Switzerland
Williams@ventures-worldwide.com
http://www.ventures-worldwide.com
http://www.peaceful-productivity.com

The growth of the self-help tradition

In the depths of the Great Depression, popular thinkers emerged to preach the gospel of self-reliance and reassert the power of the American Dream. By the mid-1930s faith in the economic system was profoundly shaken. Adding to the widespread unemployment and destitution was a paralysing fear of poverty. Whatever options were available to people at that point in history for guidance, encouragement, and insights into their individual potential, coaching was not yet one of them. Napoleon Hill and Dale Carnegie offered a new path to success through mental 're-visioning' and positive affirmations.

Carnegie's *How to Win Friends and Influence People* (first published in 1936) and Hill's *Think and Grow Rich* (first published in 1937) would inspire an American tradition of self-help gurus, including the Reverend Norman Vincent Peale, author of *The Power of Positive Thinking* (1952), Earl Nightingale, an inspirational speaker who recorded *The Strangest Secret* (1956) – the first spoken-word recording to sell over half a million copies – and Maxwell Maltz, a plastic surgeon, who promised to heal inner scars through his astoundingly popular book, *Psycho-Cybernetics: A new way to get more living out of life* (1960). Self-help publishing is now a worldwide phenomenon. If you search on Amazon.co.uk for self-help books you'll have over 128,000 to choose from. Amazon.com offers over 165,000. My guess is that they are not all saying different things. The best of them find fresh ways of expressing old insights.

Napoleon Hill: positive thinking for material gain

Napoleon Hill (1883–1970) grew up in poverty. He was born in a one room cabin in the Appalachian town of Pound in south-west Virginia. His mother died when he was 10. At the age of 13, he began writing as a 'mountain reporter' for small-town newspapers in Wise County, Virginia.

In 1908, when he was 25, Hill was assigned to interview industrialist Andrew Carnegie as part of a series of articles about famous and successful men. Carnegie was impressed with Hill and asked him to interview and analyse over 500 successful men and women. Hill interviewed an impressive list, including Henry Ford, Charles M. Schwab, Theodore Roosevelt, Wilbur Wright, William Jennings Bryan, Woodrow Wilson, William H. Taft, Luther Burbank, Alexander Graham Bell, Thomas Edison, F. W. Woolworth and Clarence Darrow. The result of this research was a study course called *Law of Success*, which Hill later developed into a book.

Think and Grow Rich (1937) was based on the *Law of Success* and proposed 13 principles which, followed diligently, would produce both wealth and personal satisfaction through being a good person. Success, according to Hill, comes when you control your mind's perception of yourself. If you believe you can succeed at a goal, you will. Hill adds credibility to his argument by illustrating it with stories of success, citing the experiences of some of his more famous interviewees. He asserts that the same kind of mental power is accessible to all people: 'Remember, no more effort is required to aim high in life, to demand abundance and prosperity, than is required to accept misery and poverty' (Hill 2009: 38).

Weak politics and strong psychology

There is a political dimension to Hill's views. The world will become a fairer place, he believes, if all people do their share and give as well as take. His emphasis on sturdy independence and self-reliance allows no room for union action or collective bargaining:

> Business is due for a reform, make no mistake about this! The methods of the past, based upon economic combinations of force and fear, will be supplanted by the better principles of faith and cooperation. Men who labor will receive more than daily wages; they will receive dividends from the business, the same as those who supply the capital for business; but, first they must give more to their employers, and stop this bickering and bargaining by force, at the expense of the public. *They must earn the right to dividends.* (Hill 2009: 93)

Hill would be more convincing on this point if he could tell us how this transformation in business practices would come about, and if he could explain why it is the workers who must take the first step by renouncing what little power they have, before expecting the employers to reciprocate. In his politics, Hill follows the tradition of Samuel Smiles, the nineteenth-century Scottish radical who gave up campaigning for socialist reforms to promote the idea of self-improvement for the working classes in his book *Self-Help*, published in 1859.

When it comes to the psychological dimension of personal success, Hill's thinking is more sophisticated. His 13 principles include organized planning, imagination, persistence, and specialized knowledge. Each of these is a 'step to riches'. In keeping with the promise of the book's title, he puts some form of mental control at the heart of all these principles. He advocates a burning desire to win (essential to success), the importance of faith and prayer, and an intentional dwelling on creative thoughts.

Hill encouraged his readers to read the book three times, and return repeatedly to individual chapters. He advocated the formation of what he called 'master mind groups', who would gather regularly to help one another achieve his principles. This showed a characteristic combination of self-belief and marketing know-how. It was also audacious: this kind of cooperative home study was more usually reserved for the Bible. In marketing terms at least, Hill's self-confidence was justified. By the time he died in 1970 *Think and Grow Rich* had sold 20 million copies and been translated into several dozen languages.

In his later life, like many people who reach a certain age having achieved success, Hill began to concentrate on quality of life issues. In his eighties he published a book called *Grow Rich with Peace of Mind*. But the spiritual dimension had always been significant in his thinking:

> New readers of *Think and Grow Rich* are often surprised at the extent of its metaphysical or spiritual concepts, yet it is these that buttress Hill's claim that the book was indeed a philosophical work. Of course its chief aim was to advance and enrich its readers, but as Max Weber demonstrated in his famous essay, spiritual and material goals can go together. Not only this, but combining them was part of the American way of life. (Butler-Bowden in Hill 2009: 15)

Dale Carnegie: the benefit of understanding others

Like Hill, Dale Carnegie (1888–1955) grew up in poor circumstances. He worked as a child, and was able to obtain a college education. After college, he moved to New York intending to be an actor, but ended up living at the YMCA on 125th Street in New York. He persuaded the manager to allow him to teach public speaking, but discovered that he could fulfil a broader purpose:

> I have, since 1912, been conducting educational courses for business and professional men and women in New York. At first, I conducted courses in public speaking only … But gradually, as the seasons passed, I realized that as sorely as these adults needed training in effective speaking, they needed still more training in the fine art of getting along with people in everyday business and social contacts. (Carnegie 1998: 15)

One of Carnegie's successful marketing moves was to change the spelling of his last name from the Irish 'Carnagey' to Carnegie at a time when Andrew Carnegie, to whom he was not related, was a widely revered and recognized name.

How to Win Friends and Influence People grew directly from his teaching. In a simple, down-to-earth style, he proposes wise techniques for working with people, making them like you, winning them to your way of thinking, and changing them without giving offence or arousing resentment. His advice includes the following admirably intelligent precepts:

Try to understand the other person's point of view: Remember that other people may be totally wrong. But they don't think so. Don't condemn them. Any fool can do that. Try to understand them. Only wise, tolerant, exceptional people even try to do that. (Carnegie 1998: 171)

Don't criticize, condemn, or complain: Instead of condemning people, let's try to understand them. Let's try to figure out why they do what they do. That's a lot more profitable and intriguing than criticism; and it breeds sympathy, tolerance and kindness . . . (Carnegie 1998: 40)

Carnegie advocates that we should give honest and sincere appreciation to others, concentrating on their good points, and think less of our own accomplishments and needs. He asks us not to promise anything we can't deliver and to concentrate on the benefits to others of our behaviour.

The Carnegie philosophy and training

The training course, which is still alive today, consists of a five-phase improvement cycle:

1. Build greater self-confidence.
2. Strengthen people skills.
3. Enhance communication skills.
4. Develop leadership skills.
5. Improve our attitude and reduce stress.

Carnegie drew on his acting background and his practical experience as an educator to develop radical teaching methods. Participants talked in groups, made personal reports, engaged in role-playing exercises and undertook group tasks. The training, which continues to this day, still uses these techniques and follows Carnegie's advice in offering praise and positive reinforcement. Some of Carnegie's behaviour modification techniques anticipate strategies developed by Aaron Beck in cognitive behavioural therapy.

Among Carnegie's many ideas, perhaps the most essential is the importance of trying to see things from the other person's point of view:

If, as a result of reading this book, you get only one thing – an increased tendency to think always in terms of the other person's point of view, and see things from that person's angle, as well as your own – if you get only one thing from this book, it may easily prove to be one of the stepping-stones of your career. (Carnegie 1998: 175)

Carnegie was identifying a capacity whose importance is recognized in the field of adult development. The capacity of see things from another's perspective is one of the features of higher levels of development. If only the process of helping someone to achieve this were as simple as Carnegie makes it sound.

Alcoholics Anonymous: the limits of individual control

While Hill and Carnegie were holding out the promise of success as a reward for self-control, self-belief, and the effective cultivation of relationships, two remarkable individuals – Bill Wilson and Bob Smith – were tackling one of the most widespread causes of failure.

Bill Wilson (1895–1971) was raised by his grandparents and grew up in poor circumstances in East Dorset, Vermont. After serving in the military, he had a promising career on Wall Street, but his drinking ruined his relationships and his business chances. He was hospitalized numerous times for alcoholism, but kept going back to the bottle. On a business trip in Akron, Ohio, he met Bob Smith (1871–1950), a fellow alcoholic, and the two began a relationship which would last throughout their lives. First they helped each other to stay sober, and then developed a programme of self-help for other recovering alcoholics. Alcoholics Anonymous was founded in 1935. Adopting the anonymous style of its members, the founders became known, and are known to this day, as Bill W. and Dr Bob.

Today, Alcoholics Anonymous has a membership of approximately 2 million people worldwide. The 'bible' of the organization, also called *Alcoholics Anonymous* and commonly known as *The Big Book*, has sold over 30 million copies. In 2011, *Time* magazine placed the book in its list of 100 best and most influential books written in English since 1923, and Bill W. one of the most influential figures in history.

Alcoholics Anonymous has been studied by organization specialists for years, because of its unique structure and its ability to endure over time. AA groups are self-supporting and are neither businesses nor charities. There are no dues or membership fees. Groups rely on voluntary membership donations. There is no hierarchical leadership and no member of the organization is allowed to contribute more than $3,000 per year. AA returns contributions mailed from outside sources. The organizational principles of AA have been adopted for use by other groups, including Narcotics Anonymous, Overeaters Anonymous, and Al-Anon, a group for family members of alcoholics.

AA's guiding principles

In AA, the effort to maintain a state of sobriety, a very specific change in behaviour, is accomplished through a series of 12 steps. Written as first-person narrative, they outline the AA process of becoming and staying sober.

1. We admitted we were powerless over alcohol – that our lives had become unmanageable.
2. Came to believe that a Power greater than ourselves could restore us to sanity.
3. Made a decision to turn our will and our lives over to the care of God as we understood Him.
4. Made a searching and fearless moral inventory of ourselves.
5. Admitted to God, to ourselves, and to another human being the exact nature of our wrongs.
6. Were entirely ready to have God remove all these defects of character.
7. Humbly asked Him to remove our shortcomings.
8. Made a list of all persons we had harmed, and became willing to make amends to them all.
9. Made direct amends to such people wherever possible, except when to do so would injure them or others.
10. Continued to take personal inventory and when we were wrong promptly admitted it.
11. Sought through prayer and meditation to improve our conscious contact with God as we understood Him, praying only for knowledge of His will for us and the power to carry that out.
12. Having had a spiritual awakening as the result of these steps, we tried to carry this message to alcoholics and to practise these principles in all our affairs.

Central to the organization's principles is the importance of helping other alcoholics in need and the compassionate understanding of alcoholism. Bill W. is quoted talking to a woman arriving at an AA meeting in 1943: 'We have a physical allergy and a psychological compulsion. We can't tolerate it, but we're compelled to drink. You can't help this. You're not bad, you're sick' (Robertson 1988: 82). Though still somewhat controversial, the understanding of alcoholism as a disease is widely accepted.

AA has adopted a version of what has come to be known as the Serenity Prayer, written in the 1930s by the theologian Reinhold Neibuhr: 'God, grant me the serenity to accept the things I cannot change, courage to change the things I can, and wisdom to know the difference.' Central to AA's approach is the importance of taking 'one day at a time'.

It is remarkable to consider the insights of these men in their historical context. Though some of their attitudes and some of what they advocated might seem old fashioned and patriarchal, their wisdom stands out. The best of what they promoted anticipated concepts that would be elaborated later in humanistic psychology, in the human potential movement, and that we would inherit in our work as coaches.

Implications for coaching

The huge number of self-help books currently available suggests that they answer a need. The emphasis has shifted from the political or moral dimensions of self-reliance to the individual search for happiness, serenity and success, but many of the key ideas of the early gurus still resonate. As coaches we are all, in a sense, in the self-help business, and these ideas commonly surface in our work:

1. Forgiving oneself and others is essential to healthy growth. As a coach, help your client enhance her belief in herself. Self-belief is essential to true serenity.
2. For some clients, faith is an important ingredient in the process of personal growth and having a spiritual orientation makes it easier to face the challenges of living.
3. Becoming rich will not necessarily produce happiness. Help your client understand that there may be more important things in life than material wealth.
4. Help your client understand that success in any aspect of life involves the ability to understand the other person's point of view.
5. Remember to give honest and sincere appreciation to your client and encourage her to do the same with others.
6. Don't promise anything to your clients that you can't deliver.
7. Central to healthy living is the value of apologizing and making amends to people you may have harmed.

Chapter 2: On the edge: human potential and the Esalen Institute

While *humanistic psychology* set the stage for establishing the coach–client relationship, the *human potential movement* put it into action. I stand on the shoulders of giants, being trained and influenced by many who shaped the human potential movement including Will Schutz, Michael Murphy, Bob Tannenbaum, and disciples of Carl Rogers, Virginia Satir, Fritz Perlz and more. Their principles of human potential and experimentation have expanded my mind and my being. They reside in my DNA and guide my work with my clients.

I'm reminded of what attracted me to say 'yes' to a potential new client who wanted to hire me for a six-month executive coaching engagement. He said that he wanted to develop himself as a leader. This may sound mundane or clichéd, but he was sincere. He is successful in his career. His company doesn't expect him to further develop as an executive; he was already doing outstanding work. Yet he wanted to continue to grow and develop as a leader and human being. I said yes. Why? Because he demonstrated the key qualities that I consider pillars of a bridge to a successful executive coaching engagement and coach–client relationship:

1. willingness (to experiment, learn, grow and develop)
2. ability to gain new insights (about himself and the impact of his thinking and actions), and
3. accountability (holding himself accountable for his choices and actions).

Consistent with the human potential movement, I too must hold myself accountable for supporting his growth and development in a way that I am willing to learn and grow and to gain new insights about myself.

When I work with clients, I am constantly reminded of one of the most important 'themes' that I gained from my involvement and knowledge of the human potential movement: Our responsibility – as coaches and as clients – is to take responsibility for ourselves. Once we own our shortcomings and virtues, we can stand beside, rather than above, our clients and conduct our life and work as coaches, both ethically and with compassion for others.

Laura Hauser, PhD, PCC
Santa Clara, California, USA
Leadership Strategies International
laura@leadership-strategies.com
www.leadership-strategies.com

We are all in the gutter, but some of us are looking at the stars.

Oscar Wilde

A time of creative turmoil

On 1 February 1960, four black students from Agricultural and Technical College, in Greensboro, North Carolina sat down in the 'whites only' section of a Woolworth's lunch counter and refused to leave. This took extraordinary courage. Since the Civil War, the system of racial segregation in the southern states of America was enforced by a spectrum of powers that ranged from the forces of law to acts of individual violence, intimidation, and even murder. The next day 24 students returned to join the demonstration. By 7 February there were 54 sit-ins throughout the south in 15 cities and 9 states. Within a few months it is estimated that 70,000 people, both black and white, were sitting down in 'whites only' sections of lunch counters all over the South. By July of that year, Woolworths had integrated its lunch counters.

These sit-ins were not centrally directed. They didn't follow a prearranged strategy. The courage and determination to oppose an oppressive system proved to be contagious and the resistance to it grew spontaneously. It was an explosion of empowerment and it galvanized the country and the watching world.

Some drew from it a directly political message. In 1962 a group of students gathered in Port Huron, Michigan to write a document that would prove influential in radical and progressive politics of the time. The Port Huron Statement, out of which grew Students for a Democratic Society (SDS), cited in its introduction 'the Southern struggle against racial bigotry' as the event that had compelled its authors 'from silence to activism'. This was a key moment in the birth of the New Left. SDS engaged in community organizing in poor neighbourhoods and went on to become the leading force in opposing the Vietnam War.

Meanwhile, at the Esalen Institute in Big Sur, California, people were gathering to discuss the possibilities for human growth. These events – the Civil Rights movement and the rise of student activism in the political realm, and these new explorations of human potential in the psychological and spiritual realm – were all part of a moment in history. For a whole range of reasons, new possibilities for people were emerging. At the heart of all of these movements was the idea that human beings could be greater, achieve more freedom, and accomplish more than had been commonly imagined.

Esalen flourished during one of those periods of intellectual and social ferment when people are thrown together in unprecedented ways and their onward lives take unpredictable paths. Barriers were broken down. Gender roles were challenged, settled structural arrangements disrupted, moral lines redrawn. Esalen, a centre of particularly intense psychological and spiritual experimentation, served as a prism, taking in light and refracting it in many directions.

The founders of the Esalen Institute, Richard Price and Michael Murphy, had been contemporaries at Stanford, where they had both studied with Frederick Spiegelberg, a professor of comparative religion and Indic studies, but did not meet until later. Price had gone on to read psychology at Harvard and serve in the Air Force. In San Francisco, he encountered the British philosopher Alan Watts, who was a major figure in introducing westerners to Zen Buddhism and other branches of Eastern philosophy and religion. Another profound influence on Price was a lecture delivered by the novelist Aldous Huxley on 'human potentialities'. Huxley argued that there was:

> reason for tempered optimism that there are still a great many potentialities – for rationality, for affection and kindliness, for creativity – still lying latent in man . . . The neurologists have shown us that no human being has ever made use of as much as ten per cent of all the neurons in his brain. And perhaps, if we set about it in a right way, we might be able to produce extraordinary things out of this strange piece of work that a man is. ('Human Potentialities', lecture delivered at the University of California, San Francisco Medical Center, 1960)

Around this time, Price was introduced to Michael Murphy, who had returned from an Ashram in India. Together they decided to form a centre which would explore and promote the idea that there might be significant dimensions of undeveloped human potential. As well as Huxley and Watts, they were influenced by the beat poets, particularly Alan Ginsberg. They chose Big Sur, where Murphy's family had land, an area of benign climate and striking natural beauty, with natural hot springs, overlooking the Pacific Ocean.

New ways of learning

Esalen opened its doors in 1962 with a workshop led by Alan Watts. A variety of workshops followed on topics such as 'Individual Cultural Definitions of Rationality' and 'Drug-Induced Mysticism'. Initially these workshops were intellectual in emphasis, and were designed to lead to a form of cognitive enlightenment. People gathered to talk, discuss and debate. From the beginning Price and Murphy wanted this to be a place of open exploration, not committed to one leader or one philosophy. An important contributor to the early thinking was Abraham Maslow, who had just published *Toward a Psychology of Being* that year. It became required reading for many of the Esalen workshops. The book was a breakthrough in the field of human potential:

> *Toward a Psychology of Being* was one of those books that goes around changing people's lives. Like Frederick Perls' *Gestalt Therapy*, the book that Aldous Huxley and Alan Watts often recommended in their lectures, it was talked about, passed along from person to person, cherished, read, and remembered. (Anderson 2004: 66)

As Esalen developed, offering an increasing number of programmes, the emphasis broadened from meetings where people discussed issues, to more experiential activities. Workshops began exploring what was happing inside the group; how people reacted; what issues got raised; and how people handled the group experience.

The concept of group dynamics was not new. The term had been coined by Kurt Lewin in the 1940s (Chapter 11). Lewin had worked at the Tavistock Clinic in London, seeking to understand the phases through which groups develop, how individual roles are chosen or assigned, the patterns of leadership, and the way decisions are made. Out of this came the sensitivity training group or T-group, often known as the encounter group, with its explicit educational purpose of enlightening individuals on how their behaviour in the group affects others and how the behaviour of others affects them. These experiments were developed by Lewin himself and others at the National Training Laboratories, headquartered in Bethel, Main, where their work continues today.

This was a revolutionary procedure – to bring people together purely for the purpose of confronting them with the complexity of their reactions to each other and the impact even their most subtle and unconscious behaviours had on others. If there was a precedent for such an encounter – a meeting structured only in its outer limits of time and place, but otherwise without an explicit agenda and with no content for its members to consider except what arose within it – it was perhaps in a Friends Meeting House where people speak as the spirit moves them. But such unprogrammed Quaker meetings put an emphasis on silence; there is an expectation that people will pause between one contribution and the next, precisely to discourage argument or confrontation. At a more profound level, the precedent for what is set up in the controlled laboratory environment of a supervised encounter group is the life of the family and, by extension, of the workplace, and of society itself, where people are thrust together, and not always in the calming presence of God. Carl Rogers reportedly described the T-group as 'the most significant social invention of the century'.

Encounters with Will Schutz and Fritz Perls

As encounter groups of various kinds became a staple of the work at Esalen, one of the most influential figures to emerge was Will Schutz (1925–2002). He had been a professor at Harvard, where he developed the *Firo-B* instrument in its earliest form (Chapter 16). Schutz had decided to give up academia and make his way to Esalen, where he would have to raise his own salary by attracting participants. His dream was to bring people together, not only for the purpose of self-understanding, but also for understanding our 'oneness' with each other:

> When people are regarded superficially their differences are accentuated – black and white, male and female, aggressive and passive, intellectual and emotional, happy and sad, radical and reactionary. But as we understand each other, differences fade and the oneness of man emerges – the same needs, the same fears, the same struggles, and the same desires. Here comes everybody. (Schutz 1971: xii)

Schutz had undertaken a series of body experiences including Rolfing (a revolutionary form of physical therapy). He added a physical element to the encounter group, claiming that 'virtually any feeling has a physical counterpart' (Schutz 1971: 172). People in the group were encouraged to express their emotions, not only through words, but also through physical gestures. Nudity became part of the group process. Sometimes one person within the group was encouraged to remove his or her clothes. At other times, the entire group disrobed and spent time talking or relaxing naked with each other.

> Why do these methods work? . . . Joy derives from realizing potential. What potential is it that these methods help the individual to realize? Perhaps it's the potential for being more of a person than I thought I could be; for being more significant, competent, and lovable; for being a more meaningful individual, capable of coping more effectively with the world and better able to give and receive love. (Schutz 1967: 219)

Another major influence at Esalen was Fritz Perls (Chapter 8), who spent his later years there, a revered presence, youthful in spite of his age. Fritz was always controversial, often sarcastic, but fiercely insightful. A group session with Fritz Perls was a mixed bag. Some feared and disliked him. Others considered him a genius. His approach to group therapy was experimental, challenging, and never dull. He represented the spirit of the place. In a meeting with Maslow and other Esalen dignitaries, Perls demonstrated gestalt behaviour in the extreme. In the middle of this somewhat stilted meeting:

> Fritz slid down from his chair onto the floor . . . and the whole group watched in horrified silence as Fritz slithered across the floor toward the philosopher [Maslow], reached one supplicating arm toward him and said, 'Come down here with the rest of us; get down with the common people.' Maslow told Fritz he was being childish, so Fritz proceeded to be childish in gestalt therapy style: do it all the way, invest yourself in it, get fully in touch with it. He crawled around on the floor and made whining sounds and hugged Maslow's knees. There sat kindly Maslow, a professor at Brandeis, the father of humanistic psychology, rigid as a rock in this crew cut and cashmere sweater while this crazy old man in a jumpsuit hugged his knees and made baby noises. 'This begins to look like sickness,' Maslow said. (Anderson 2004: 136)

A convergence of remarkable thinkers

Esalen was becoming an epicentre of 1960s social revolution. Literally 'on the edge', perched on steep hills high above the Pacific Ocean, it attracted people who wanted to push the boundaries of the self and break free of society's constraints. Here was a place where people were not only discussing the means by which the obstacles to human potential might be overcome, but opening up to their own inner potential in the process. They were forging an inclusive community that was intellectually exciting, personally challenging, and held the promise of expansive spiritual growth. As Esalen flourished and expanded, its reputation spread. It was both a physical place and a concept – a seething forum for a whole range of ideas and practices designed to expand human potential and human consciousness:

> It appealed to those who were trying to make sense of what was happening in society and to those who were interested in making more personal and immediate changes in their own lives: rediscovering their bodies, opening up their senses, learning to feel and communicate their desires. (Anderson 2004: 146)

The number and variety of influential thinkers who helped shape Esalen and taught courses there in the early years is astounding. As well as psychologists and psychotherapists, such as Fritz Perls, Carl Rogers, Abraham Maslow, Virginia Satir and B. F. Skinner, there was an eclectic mix of artists, scientists, philosophers and spiritual teachers, including Aldous Huxley, Ram Dass, Timothy Leary, Linus Pauling, Paul Tillich, Arnold Toynbee and Buckminster Fuller.

Other speakers and visitors over the years included Ida Rolf, biochemist and inventor of Rolfing, the dissident Catholic theologian Matthew Fox, anthropologist Gregory Bateson, Joseph Campbell who popularized the study of comparative mythology, free-thinking physicists Fritjof Capra, Richard Feynman and Amory Lovins, spiritual healer Deepak Chopra, psychiatrists Stanislav Grof and R. D. Laing, existential psychologist Rollo May, writer and activist Susan Sontag, Jungian psychologist and poet Marion Woodman, singer Joan Baez, photographer Ansel Adams, and Ken Kesey, author of *One Flew Over the Cuckoo's Nest*.

Capturing the moment

One individual who was influenced by Esalen was John Whitmore. Whitmore was involved in bringing concepts evolving at Esalen back to the United Kingdom and introducing people to a paradigm shift in thinking about the potential of human behaviour and change:

> I felt that what was going on in Esalen and the anti-war movement were logical outgrowths for humanity. Psychology had always been about fixing problems ... and Esalen was doing something different. These events were two crucial wake-up calls getting people to think in what I would call whole systems thinking – the interconnectedness of everything. (Sir John Whitmore, personal interview, 24 August 2011)

According to Whitmore, the inner life – one's feelings and emotions – needed to be explored and nurtured. Esalen, the human potential movement, and many of the activities around this centre, contributed substantially to the concept of working on the inner life; working on the 'self':

> I was inspired by what I experienced there, and I thought that this was a great opportunity to introduce England to what was happening at Esalen. So I made—produced and co-directed—a documentary of an encounter group run by Will Schutz and Betty Fuller to demonstrate the principles of humanistic psychology. (Whitmore, personal interview, 24 August 2011)

Without editorial comment, Whitmore's film captures a group of people in the middle of a period of intense historical transition, fumbling towards enlightenment. Engrained attitudes are challenged and participants are induced to free themselves from the restraints of their accustomed clothing – metaphorical or literal. There are raw and uncomfortable exchanges, as people are confronted with the effects they have on each other. It's fascinating to watch this film 40 years on. Against the backdrop of radical experimentation, the conventional elements show up more starkly now. The power of the leader over the participants, the power of the men over the women – the language had not yet been formulated to catch these imbalances in flight and name them.

Changing the self versus changing the world

For some people involved in politics in the 1960s, there seemed, at the time, to be a chasm between activities that could be described as 'changing the world' and those aimed at changing oneself. Founded at the moment when the southern states of America were in the midst of profound social upheaval, and with an impulse for political and socio-economic change spreading through university campuses, the human potential movement in general, and Esalen in particular, could be seen as self-indulgent and inward looking.

Many did see it this way. As the decade wore on, and political divisions cohered and intensified around the Vietnam War, Esalen came in for criticism as a mecca of self-indulgent behaviour, anti-intellectual thinking, and retreat from the social and political realities. There was an image of people gathering in hot tubs on a California hillside to examine their internal reality – the ultimate navel-gazing. Christopher Lasch, writing in the 1970s in *The Culture of Narcissism*, expressed these sentiments:

> Having no hope of improving their lives in any of the ways that matter, people have convinced themselves that what matters is psychic self-improvement: getting in touch with their feelings, eating health food, taking lessons in ballet or belly-dancing, immersing themselves in the wisdom of the East, jogging, learning how to 'relate', overcoming the 'fear of pleasure'. (Lasch 1979: 4)

But, with the passing of time, the overlaps and interconnections have come to seem more significant than the divisions. The struggle for Civil Rights was itself a search for a form of self-empowerment that went beyond the legal and political spheres. Ranged against those students, sitting at a 'whites only' lunch counter, were not only the police and the courts with their guns, batons and prison bars, and not only the entrenched prejudices of white society, but the 'mind-forged manacles' of internal limitation.

For others whose views were being shaped by the ongoing Civil Rights movement, whether or not they were directly involved in it, the raising of political consciousness went hand in hand with a more general opening of the mind and the heart. The Port Huron Statement, the founding document of Students for a Democratic Society, alongside its progressive political analysis, expresses a yearning for the same kind of inner expansion that motivated the founders of Esalen. Its authors asserted that 'We regard men as infinitely precious and possessed of unfulfilled capacities for reason, freedom, and love.' And went on to argue that 'Men have unrealized potential for self-cultivation, self-direction, self-understanding, and creativity' (http://www.h-net.org/~hst 306/documents/huron.html).

Meanwhile Esalen was responding in its own way to contemporary political concerns. Workshops tackled subjects that included war, racism, sexism, and environmental damage, as well as self-development. A concern for social structures and relationships had a clear political dimension.

> Dissatisfied with contemporary practices, they saw themselves struggling against individualistic, competitive value systems and hegemonic pursuits. They strove for individual wholeness, fulfilling relationships and a harmonious world. They believed their projects could provide a map to negotiate the fragmentation they felt in their own lives and in the world around them. Here, this communal and often utopian perspective fed dreams that helped drive social reform, changed the ways individuals understood themselves and their environment . . . (Wood 2010: 170)

Some of the explicitly political movements faced internal upheavals that revealed a crucial absence of psychological insight. Before the decade was over, SDS imploded with the rise of the Weathermen – a rigid and self-destructive cult distinctly lacking in the kind of self-awareness that might have helped them to recognize the dangers inherent in their internal power structures and the nature of their proposed revolution. But the New Left also gave rise to the women's movement, in which the search for personal empowerment linked changes in the external circumstances of political and social arrangements with internal growth of the individual.

Esalen, in its turn, was helping to shape wider social attitudes, contributing, for example, to a broader understanding of health – psychological, social and spiritual, as well as physical. And it too had things to learn about power structures. The encounter group, in its more confrontational manifestation, could be insensitive to vulnerable individuals and unconscious of imbalances of power between leader and participant and between men and women.

The emerging synthesis

As both the political and human potential movements grew and matured, the apparent rivalries and conflicts seemed less important. The 'politicos' became more interested in issues of lifestyle, personal wellness, and spirituality. The 'new-agers' increasingly challenged racial and social inequalities, and championed anti-war and environmental causes.

In the intervening years, this chasm has closed; not completely, but to a large extent. Young people today combine activities that were traditionally known as 'self-improvement' (meditation, yoga, psychological workshops) with political activism and working to help save the planet. They blend deep spiritual philosophies with demonstrating on Wall Street. Their lives are richer for this.

Esalen, and the human potential movement that surrounded it, has contributed significantly to what we, as coaches do today. The meta-ethos of coaching, for most of us, is the idea that relatively healthy people can and should be able to enjoy richer, fuller, more self-realized lives. In the words of Sir John Whitmore, 'That time and Esalen were crucial [to the coaching profession] and that is where, in a way, it all started.' As coaches, we are descendants of the best of what emerged from Esalen during those years.

Implications for coaching

1. As coaches, we assume that people want to develop and grow both personally and professionally.
2. Our work in coaching is to focus on the positive in people.
3. People's thoughts and feelings may have little or nothing to do with the situation in which they find themselves.
4. People are capable of changing their attitude and feelings, even when their current circumstances remain unchanged.
5. Changing thoughts and attitudes can result in changed behaviours. The world allows for infinite possibilities.
6. People are social creatures and need to understand the social environment in which they function.

Chapter 3: Reaching for the marvellous: spiritual and mystical contributions

Though people mean different things when they use the word *mindfulness*, for me it means observing the body, heart and mind with detachment, curiosity and even affection. As a practitioner of meditation, yoga and other wisdom traditions, I practise mindfulness to increase awareness, strengthen the mind's 'inner observer' capacity, and cultivate compassion and presence as a coach. Mindfulness is instrumental to my ability to be an effective coach.

When I place myself 'in service' to my client I create a way of being that supports client development and well-being. When I let go of attachment to my own ideas, interpretations and judgements, I can extend to my client what Carl Rogers called 'unconditional positive regard'. Intentional mindfulness practices – such as sitting and walking meditation, yoga, the creative arts – hone my capacity, over time, to make these internal shifts and help create a shared mindset of safety, acceptance, openness and respect – necessary conditions for trusting relationships and transformative change. In the context of the coaching session, maintaining mindfulness helps me recognize and manage the sensations, emotions and thoughts that arise in the moment, choose whether to put them aside or share them, and remain focused on the experiences and needs of my client.

When I offer mindfulness practices to interested clients they discover valuable resources in themselves to reduce damaging stress and expand awareness of choice and possibility. Recent findings from neuroscience and other fields confirm the benefits of mindfulness meditation for mental and physical health. This fact has only strengthened my appreciation of the value of mindfulness practices for both the coach and the client.

Janet Baldwin Anderson, PhD
Tacoma Park, Maryland, USA
JBA Coaching Services
janet@jbacoaching.com
http://www.jbacoaching.com

The yearning for spiritual renewal

Carl Rogers seemed destined for a career as a Christian minister. As a junior in college he travelled to China to take part in an international World Student Christian Federation Conference. Encountering for the first time a radically different religious tradition, he began to question the faith in which he had been raised. During his two years at Union Theological Seminary he began to forge a personal philosophy that led him to a career outside the Church.

For many in the middle years of the twentieth century, who found themselves on a spiritual quest, Eastern beliefs were a source of influence. For Rogers it was the very fact that beliefs could diverge so greatly that prompted him to question the religion he had known all his life and find his own path. Others shrank from certain kinds of puritanical rigidity, having experienced established religion as the English poet William Blake had described it in 'The Garden of Love':

> So I turned to the Garden of Love
> That so many sweet flowers bore.
> And I saw it was filled with graves,
> And tombstones where flowers should be:
> And Priests in black gowns were walking their rounds,
> And binding with briars my joys & desires.

Others found themselves uninspired by religious traditions that seemed to undervalue the miraculous and the mystical, or had grown up with the kind of religious practice that is little more than a hollow routine, an aspect of social conformism, in which lip service is paid to doctrines once experienced as profound and radical. Some were raised without religion of any kind, and with nothing else that might nurture that part of the mind or spirit that reaches for the marvellous. The time was ripe for a renewed investigation into spiritual possibilities:

> there are periods in the history of any civilization when its rest is disturbed, and in such periods the inner life runs near the surface, ordinary people crave mystical experience, there is much odd behaviour, and many things seem possible. (Anderson 2004: 8)

The new relevance of Jung

For many who found themselves on a spiritual quest, Eastern traditions became attractive. Among the founders of depth psychology, it was Carl Jung (1875–1961) (Chapter 6) who had delved most deeply into the mystical. His concept of the *collective unconscious* was profoundly at odds with scientific materialism and the Western emphasis on the individual. He too was intellectually open to all kinds of religious impulses.

> To the psychologist there is nothing more stupid than the standpoint
> of the missionary who pronounces the gods of the 'poor heathen'
> to be illusions. But unfortunately we keep blundering along in the
> same dogmatic way, as if what we call the real were not equally full of
> illusion. In psychic life, as everywhere in our experience, all things
> that act are actual, regardless of the names man chooses to bestow on
> them. (Jung 1933: 73)

As the appeal of Eastern religious and philosophical traditions grew, Jung
found new readers. In the 1960s, Jung was adopted as a guru by the new age
movement. Not least among the reasons for this was his role in promoting
the study, aiding the dissemination, and providing modern psychological
elucidations of Eastern thought.

What Jung had found in Eastern thought was an account of the developmental phases of higher consciousness. He recognized that significant psychological shifts can occur during adult life. Jungian theory suggests that midlife
can be a period of particular confusion and uncertainty out of which one
might emerge with a stronger sense of one's identity and purpose. The term
'midlife crisis', which was coined later, in 1965, by the Canadian organizational
psychologist Elliot Jaques, has entered the language to express a popularized
version of this idea.

Alan Watts: Buddhism goes West

The British writer Alan Watts (1915–1973) came to prominence as a popularizer of Eastern thought. *The Way of Zen* (1957) introduced Buddhism to
many readers in the West not previously familiar with it. In 1958 he lectured
at the Jung Institute in Zurich. Like Jung, he saw that Buddhism could
be understood as a form of psychotherapy, a perspective he developed in
Psychotherapy East and West (1961). In his essay 'The New Alchemy' (1958)
and in the book *The Joyous Cosmology* (1962), he explored human consciousness and, like Huxley, reflected on his own experiments with mind-altering
drugs.

As a boy, Watts had shown promise but was inclined to follow his own
path, and was precocious and opinionated in a way that didn't lend itself to
conventional academic success. He attended King's School, Canterbury in the
1920s and 1930s, where he found 'the religious indoctrination . . . grim and
maudlin, though retaining fascination because it had something to do with the
basic mysteries of existence' (Watts 1972: 58). He applied to read history at
Trinity College, Cambridge, but was later told that he failed to get a scholarship
because he answered an essay question on courage 'in the style of Nietzsche,
having just read his Zarathustra' (Watts 1972: 96–7). Without the financial
resources to go to university, he found work in a printing house, attached
himself to the London Buddhist Lodge, and pursued his own course of

eclectic reading. Reflecting in later years on his interest in Asian philosophy, he emphasized that it was:

> part of an individual philosophical quest. I am not interested in Buddhism or Taoism as particular entities or subjects to be studied and defined in such a way that one must avoid 'mixing up' one's thinking about Buddhism with interests in quantum theory, psychoanalysis, gestalt psychology, semantics, and aesthetics, or in an Eckhart, Goethe, Whitehead, Jung, or Krishnamurti. I feel about the academic 'subjects' just as the Balinese feel about 'Art' when they say, 'We have no Art: we just do everything as well as possible.' (Watts 1972: 259)

In 1938 Watts moved to New York and for a while undertook formal Zen training. In what might seem a surprising turn, he decided at this point to train for the Anglican priesthood and attended a theological seminary. In 1945 he was ordained and served as a priest for five years, until his unwillingness to conform to the prescribed beliefs and practices of the institution made it impossible for him to continue. In 1951 he moved to San Francisco and took a teaching job at the American Academy of Asian Studies.

Watts saw Zen Buddhism as an intuitive way of understanding life. He was no more wedded to the strict practices of Zen than he was to orthodox Christian doctrine. He resisted the role of guru, encouraging students to find their own paths. His influence on the human potential movement was unique and joyful.

> Watts became a celebrity at Esalen, blessing buildings and bathtubs, performing marriages, celebrating Episcopalian mass, invoking Buddhist prayers, delivering sermons on Eastern thought and Western psychology, and sharing his infectious, outrageous laughter and sense of play. (Wood 2010: 184)

Allen Ginsberg: Beat Generation mystic

Among those of the beat generation who were influenced by Watts was the poet Allen Ginsberg (1926–1997). As a writer, Ginsberg drew inspiration from William Blake and Walt Whitman. But he was also a student of Zen Buddhism and a leading figure in the creative ferment of artistic and intellectual activity that found a home at Esalen. Ginsberg is most famous for 'Howl', the free-wheeling, visionary poem that is credited with kick-starting the Beat movement and bringing it to international attention. Ginsberg pictures the best minds of his generation:

> angelheaded hipsters burning for the ancient heavenly connection to the starry dynamo in the machinery of night . . .

> who bared their brains to Heaven under the El and saw Mohammedan
> angels staggering on tenement roofs illuminated,
>
> who passed through universities with radiant eyes hallucinating
> Arkansas and Blake-light tragedy among the scholars of war. (Ginsberg
> 1961: lines 3–6)

At its first reading, in 1955 at the '6' Gallery in San Francisco, 'Howl' left the
audience 'standing in wonder, or cheering and wondering, but knowing at the
deepest level that a barrier had been broken, that a human voice and body
had been hurled against the harsh wall of America . . .' (Michael McClure:
http://www.poets.org/poet.php/prmPID/8). When the poem was published
the following year it was banned for obscenity. In one sense the writing of the
poem was a political act. It was also an assertion of spiritual freedom – a
vibrant expression of an inner vision unconstrained by social norms.

Aldous Huxley: opening the doors of perception

Spiritual seekers in this period found another source of inspiration in Aldous
Huxley (1894–1963), the veteran British novelist and essayist. Huxley had
been experimenting with mescaline as a means to expand consciousness.
In 1954, in his sixtieth year, Huxley's essay 'The Doors of Perception' was
published. He took his title from Blake's strange and beautiful poem, *The
Marriage of Heaven and Hell*: 'If the doors of perception were cleansed everything
would appear to man as it is: infinite' (Erdman 1988: 39). But it was Huxley's
essay that inspired a group of musicians in Los Angeles a decade later to call
themselves *The Doors*.

Huxley writes with great empathy for the mass of people who are subjected
to a cramped and unfulfilled existence:

> Most men and women lead lives at the worst so painful, at the best so
> monotonous, poor and limited that the urge to escape, the longing to
> transcend themselves if only for a few moments, is and has always
> been one of the principle appetites of the soul. Art and religion,
> carnivals and saturnalia, dancing and listening to oratory – all these
> have served, in H. G. Wells's phrase, as Doors in the Wall. (Huxley
> 2009: 62)

Huxley argues that nothing is more important than expanding human
consciousness, seeking enlightenment, gaining 'direct perception . . . of the
inner and outer worlds into which we have been born'. He writes with satirical
energy about the failure of educational and religious institutions to attend
to this project:

A catalogue, a bibliography, a definitive edition of a third-rate [poet] . . . is sure of approval and financial support. But when it comes to finding out how you and I, our children and grandchildren, may become more perceptive, more intensely aware of inward and outward reality, more open to the Spirit . . . more capable of controlling our own autonomic nervous system . . . no really respectable person in any really respectable university or church will do anything about it. (Huxley 2009: 76)

Ram Dass: a new take on old ways of living and ageing

In 1961, two young Harvard psychologists, Richard Alpert and Timothy Leary, took the project of exploring human consciousness with the aid of psychedelic chemicals into the heart of academia. Together they devised a research programme to examine the effects of psilocybin, a substance naturally present in certain kinds of mushrooms. They used a synthesized form and experimented on volunteers. The drug was legal at the time, but the programme, not surprisingly, proved controversial.

After they were fired from the university, Leary remained principally associated with the cause of psychedelics. But Alpert's life took a different course. While crediting these youthful experiments with bringing him to an initial awareness of a new way of perceiving the world and his place in it, he realized that the answer lay elsewhere. Travelling to India, he studied with a guru and was renamed Ram Dass in 1931. In one of a series of lectures, which he gave at the Menninger Foundation in 1970, he describes his spiritual evolution in everyday language:

When I was in India in the temple, I was sitting there and there was a river flowing and birds chirping . . . and I felt this great feeling of well-being and calmness and I thought, 'What am I doing here? Why aren't I back on the front lines? Why aren't I back protesting injustice? Am I copping out? Is this like a rear battle rest station?' . . . Then I began to see that staying alone in that room at that moment was confronting me with an internal battle which was much fiercer than any external battle I had ever fought before . . . I began to see that it was absolutely imperative in terms of socially responsible, effective behavior that I work on myself sufficiently so that I could look at any human being and see that place in them behind whatever their melodrama is, be it Nixon or a hippie, or Mao or Hitler . . . Until I was centered enough, I couldn't really know that place in other beings. I saw that, finally, my responsibility was to work on myself. (Ram Dass 1970: 39)

Ram Dass advocates the deep spiritual work of meditation and study for achieving a sustainable kind of enlightenment. He has written extensively, but he is probably best known for *Be Here Now*, in which he recounts his own spiritual journey and speaks with humility and humour about how to live joyously. In later writings, he tends to put the sixties experience – both its countercultural experiments and its political activism – in a compassionate but diminished perspective:

> Back in the sixties when we gathered we were confused as to whether we were psychotic or spiritual . . . And as we started to break free there was much melodrama: violence, anger, confusion, as well as bliss and delight . . . We were confused between internal freedom and external freedom, between revolution and evolution, because we didn't have models in our heads that would allow us to appreciate the grandeur of the change that we were undergoing. So we kept reducing its implications and seeing it as a social, psychological, or political change. (Ram Dass 1987: 19)

After Alan Watts, Ram Dass has probably done more than anyone to make Eastern thought – particularly Hinduism – accessible to a Western public. In his later lectures and writings, he talks about the advantages of ageing and the concept of a 'self' separate from the physical body. He describes holding his mother as she died and the gift of the connection between mother and son, as they helped each other through this final passage.

In 1997 Ram Dass suffered a major stroke. After intensive physical therapy, he has been able to return to lecturing. The title of his latest book, *Still Here*, reflects his ironic and light touch on life, death, and the capacity for experiencing each day as a blessing:

> Recently, a friend said to me, 'You're more human since the stroke than you were before.' This touched me profoundly. What a gift the stroke has given me, to finally learn that I don't have to renounce my humanity in order to be spiritual – that I can be both witness and participant, both eternal spirit and aging body. (Ram Dass 2000: 7)

Ram Dass has been central to the growth of many seeking more serenity and joy, myself included.

Democratizing spirituality

The mid-twentieth-century injection of Eastern philosophy and mysticism into Western culture had a huge and lasting impact, extending options for religious belief, popularizing practices such as yoga and meditation, and generally shaking up attitudes. It also encouraged a re-examination of neglected areas of Western thought. Writing in the 1980s, co-founder of Esalen, Michael Murphy, and Esalen veteran and humanistic psychologist George Leonard, argued that this 'soul-awakening from the East is complemented today by the rediscovery of Western esoteric traditions':

> As well as Sufism, cabalistic and Hasidic mysticism, and certain aspects of Islam, the words of Christian mystics are being published in record numbers. The early desert fathers, Orthodox Greek and Russian saints, medieval mystics such as Hildegarde of Bingen and Meister Eckhart, the Spanish ascetics St Teresa of Avila and St John of the Cross, Protestant ecstatics such as Jakob Böhme and George Fox, and other God-intoxicated people of ancient, medieval, and modern Christendom influence us today through their newly translated writings, their vivid examples of holy life, and their imaginative ways of self-transcendence. (Leonard and Murphy 1995: xv)

All this has added to what might be called the democratization of spirituality. People feel freer to acknowledge a spiritual dimension in their lives, to explore and express religious impulses, without having to subscribe to any particular doctrine or become paid-up members of any organization. Religions, and sects within religions, often come to be defined by what separates them – by what, in business, would be called their unique selling points. The spirituality movement, in contrast, focuses on overlapping insights and shared wisdom.

The American priest and theologian Matthew Fox, who was silenced by the Vatican, expelled from the Dominican order in 1993 for his unorthodox writings, and subsequently received into the Episcopal Church, is a leading thinker in the field of deep ecumenism. His books include *Original Blessing: A Primer in Creation Spirituality* (1983), *The Reinvention of Work: A new vision of livelihood for our time* (1993), and *One River, Many Wells* (2000), in which he explores the idea that the various religious traditions are different manifestations of the same underlying spiritual truths.

Implications for coaching

Coaches commonly work with clients who are relatively well adjusted, and often relatively successful, helping them to become more emotionally healthy, more focused, more centred, more joyful, more of who they are when they are being their best selves. Whether or not spirituality enters the conversation explicitly – that is, whether or not it is part of the client's conceptual framework – all of this 'moreness' could be understood as part of the spiritual dimension of being alive and responding creatively and with serenity to what life brings up.

1. Finding more spiritual meaning in life is a common theme in coaching conversations. Helping your client to discuss what spirituality means to her can be enormously helpful.
2. It is important to be sensitive to your client's spiritual and religious beliefs. These can be intensely personal matters. At the same time, don't be afraid to let the client talk about them in her own terms.
3. Be aware of your own beliefs around spirituality and spiritual practices, and make sure they don't intrude inappropriately.
4. Spiritual traditions are a rich source of wisdom for day-to-day living and include techniques for coping with stress and anxiety, and ways of focusing on the larger context to put problems in perspective. You can pass on such skills to your client in whatever language works for her.
5. When you are focused on your client's agenda – concentrating deeply on who she is and what she is saying – you are engaging in a form of meditation. This in itself can be deeply healing for your client in addition to enhancing your own capacity to relax and concentrate.

Chapter 4: Marketing transformation: from *est* to NLP

The term *neuro-linguistic programming* (NLP), since the mid 70s, has been associated with personal change. I was in Cambridge, England, when I first saw the words as part of the title to a book on training, and it took me several reads to 'get it'. I trained for 40 days over nine months to become a Master Practitioner, used the title with pride, and soon realized I was uncannily good at it. I had no idea where its roots were philosophically, just that people tended to say things like 'If it works, its NLP.'

As I looked into NLP's origins I was less happy, finding out that it really did have a strong, almost quasi-religious base. It wasn't just a set of clever techniques, but had all sorts of 'presuppositions', most of which were fine, but some of which made me feel uncomfortable. I certainly don't believe that 'everyone has all of the resources they need' because we need resources beyond ourselves or we die; nor that 'if one person can do something, anyone else can learn to do it.'

Features I *do* like and practise include its emphasis on language. I make clients aware of how their language affects their behaviour, and as they gain more insight they change. People who use Universal Quantifiers, for instance – *all, everyone, nothing, never, completely* – often feel the pendulum of their emotions swinging wildly. People who move away from 'UQs' can become more emotionally stable. We also use questions like, 'When you have X (the Desired Outcome), what will that give you?' That question takes people to a completely different level.

Andrew Sercombe
West Sussex, United Kingdom
andrew@powerchange.com
http://www.powerchange.com

The Werner Erhard story

When Jack Rosenberg decided to become Werner Erhard in his mid-twenties, he wasn't just changing his name; he was reinventing himself. He had left Pennsylvania, walking out on his wife and four children, and moved to Saint Louis:

> To hold the circumstances, the suffering, the horror of life at bay, I thought that one needed competence and excellence, that one needed to be 'smart'. I suppose I had in mind the building of a kind of fortress of competence. In Saint Louis I began to build that fortress. Jack Rosenberg had screwed up his life. Werner Erhard was going to do it right.' (Bartley 1978: 61–2)

Rosenberg had married his pregnant girlfriend a few weeks after his eighteenth birthday. He became a car salesman and proved to be extremely good at it, but felt trapped and intellectually thwarted. In the evenings he would read in an effort to educate himself, but also to escape: 'There was the world of making it, in which one earned a living and raised a family. Then there was that private world that made the other tolerable.' An affair with a woman called June Bryde led him to a crisis. He began to suffer alarming physical symptoms. Pulling into a parking lot he blacked out at the wheel of his car. His doctor referred him to a Freudian psychoanalyst. During the course of this treatment, he asked his wife Pat, who was pregnant with their fourth child, for a divorce. Discovering the affair, Pat confronted June and told her divorce was out of the question.

Feeling trapped, with the affair apparently over, 'not knowing which way to go, and all the time this emptiness, this death', Rosenberg reached out to June, and they eventually agreed on a radical step; they would create false identities, disappear and begin life anew.

In its broad outline, it's an archetypal story. H. G. Wells tells one version of it in *The History of Mr Polly*. Ann Tyler tells another in *Earthly Possessions*. It's the story of Dick Wittington, and of the lady who runs off 'with the wraggle taggle gypsies, oh'.

The elemental move that turned Jack Rosenberg into Werner Erhard might serve as a metaphor for the kind of psychological transformation, the leap into a new life, that Erhard came later to promote. Life for Werner and Ellen, as they had now become, was a struggle at first, but Erhard soon talked his way into jobs. He sold correspondence courses, Encyclopedia Britannica's *Great Books*, and *Parents* magazine, first in the Midwest and later in California. He was a brilliant, charismatic salesman, and soon rose to the top of the *Parents* magazine organization.

Throughout this time, Erhard kept reading and studying. He was strongly influenced by *Think and Grow Rich* by Napoleon Hill and *Psycho-Cybernetics* by Maxwell Maltz. Impressed by Dale Carnegie's self-help classic, *How to Win Friends and Influence People*, he took the Carnegie training (Chapter 1). He studied Maslow and Rogers (Chapter 9); attended the encounter and gestalt sessions at Esalen (Chapter 2); took courses in transactional analysis (Chapter 10); embarked on the enlightenment intensive, and did a quick course in Zen consciousness.

The *est* phenomenon

Erhard began attending seminars given by Alan Watts in his houseboat in Sausalito. According to Erhard, 'Watts did two main things for me . . . He opened up the connections between what I was doing and the traditional Oriental philosophies. And he pointed me toward the distinction between Self and Mind.' The Self is the source of satisfaction, Erhard concluded, while the Mind is the source of success. He was already seeking to create a training which would combine the two. In late 1971, he held the first *est* (Erhard Seminars Training) session at a hotel in San Francisco. In the view of the social psychologist Walter Anderson:

> Erhard had done his homework. He had chewed his way through a large piece of what, though we rarely recognize it as such, is as much our cultural heritage as Shakespeare or calculus: the sometimes respectable, sometimes not, ideas and practices having to do with mobilizing the human psyche toward personal success in the world of business. (Anderson 2004: 255)

Est took off immediately and within a short period of time seminars were being conducted around the world. The *est* seminar wasn't a lecture in any conventional sense; but it wasn't an encounter group either: there was explicit content and the participants encountered each other only through the constant mediation of the trainer. It was a hybrid form that seemed to strike a fresh note.

As Anderson points out, Werner Erhard's most significant contribution to the human potential movement was to Americanize it in a way that Esalen or other self-improvement groups had never done or tried to do. Before *est*, the movement's message was communicated through Zen books, researched tracts, encounter groups, hot tubs and nature (Chapter 2). Erhard's training took place in hotel ballrooms. Assistants were dressed in business clothes. The training itself was culled from the wisdom of Freud, Jung and Reich, among others. What made it unique, in addition to the business-like atmosphere, was that Erhard grafted personal and financial success on to the human potential movement. Self-help, positive thinking and personal success were all part of the *est* training. Drawing on eastern religious concepts, Erhard Americanized the language. The training consciously avoided using words such as 'enlightenment'. Instead, having an experience as a result of the training was termed 'getting it'. The language, physical atmosphere, and adherence to rules and norms served to create an experience that appealed to many people who might not otherwise have explored the human potential traditions. It also proved an effective business model.

Controversy and scandal

Many aspects of the *est* training were positive. Erhard took basic concepts from psychology, spirituality and self-help, and packaged them in a form that many people could relate to, understand and derive benefit from. The training itself employed clever ways of helping people shift their thinking towards a more positive, self-loving framework.

Other aspects, however, were harder to defend. The strict control of bathroom breaks was only the physical manifestation of a more subtle psychological tyranny. First there was the explicit premise of the training that if you didn't 'get it', failed to feel enlightened or inspired, this was your problem. On the other hand, if you did get it, this was due to the training's unique approach. It followed from this that what everyone needed, whether they'd 'got it' or not, was more *est*. Each training would end with the newly enlightened participants being encouraged – some would say pressured – to sign up for further, more advanced training. As Anderson experienced it:

> The training turned out to be a loosely assembled smorgasbord of many different methods and techniques. There were 'processes', exercises somewhat resembling psychodrama or role-playing, long lectures, periods of 'sharing' when participants talked about their personal problems, occasional confrontations when a participant was mercilessly browbeaten by the trainer for saying something unacceptable such as: 'Why don't we take a break and go have a cup of coffee?' (Anderson 2004: 82)

Erhard's involvement in the business ended in allegations and lawsuits relating to his personal and professional life. Some of the more explosive allegations were later retracted, but a sense of scandal lingered. In 1991, the intellectual property was sold to a group of *est* trainers who repackaged it as Landmark Education.

Landmark and the rebranding of *est*

In the Landmark Forum, the essential aspects of *est* live on in a modified form. It no longer makes such a virtue of aggressive confrontation. With the founding 'genius' out of the picture, Landmark is less open to the charge of being a cult, though it continues to attract criticism on these lines.

Landmark's defence is persuasive: whereas a cult depends on separating its recruits from family, friends and the wider world, it is central to the Landmark training that participants are urged to make phone calls to people in their lives with whom they have unfinished emotional business. Recipients of these make-up calls are commonly parents, partners and family members, though they might also be friends or business associates. There is an element of secrecy, certainly, in that trainers ask participants not to reveal the apparently unique 'technology' of the training to others on the grounds that it would weaken its impact, but in other respects participants are encouraged to be as open as possible about the changes they have experienced.

Landmark would not have achieved its current level of success if the contents of its training were not psychologically and spiritually smart. Essentially it promotes the idea that transformation is possible and that the crucial steps are, first, to take responsibility for one's life, and then to imagine and articulate a new possibility for yourself. As a participant you learn that there's a difference between what happens to you and the 'story', the meaning you impose on it; an attachment to what you're good at, your 'strong suit', can be as limiting in its own way as being attached to a narrative of failure, weakness or suffering, your 'racket'; your experience of life and your freedom to be your best self are diminished by unnecessary fear of others and the need to avoid humiliation; your life is richer if you 'choose' or joyfully embrace circumstances over which you have no choice; and it's liberating to communicate with people with whom you have unresolved conflicts, to express forgiveness and acknowledge responsibility.

None of this would be so effective if it were not delivered as a participatory group experience. One of the most effective insights behind the *est*/Landmark process is that, as social creatures, we create our reality in relationship with other people. Just as we draw others into our destructive narratives, so we must, in the language of Landmark, enrol them in the new possibilities we are creating for ourselves.

Neuro-linguistic programming

Unlike *est*, the seeds of neuro-linguistic programming were sown in an academic setting, but like *est* it sprouted and flourished in the marketplace. In the early 1970s Richard Bandler, an undergraduate at UC Santa Cruz in California, was studying the strategies of respected therapists, including Fritz Perls and Virginia Satir. A student of Gregory Bateson, he brought an anthropological mindset to these observations: he was interested in analysing the nature of the exchange without reference to the psychological theory or methodological assumptions underlying it.

He enlisted John Grinder, an assistant professor of linguistics. Grinder was influenced by Noam Chomsky's theory that people are born already hardwired with deep grammatical structures. Bandler and Grinder shared a postmodern outlook, and were inclined to question the idea that there was such a thing as scientific truth, or even objective reality.

What began as a linguistic model, a meta-model for effective interaction with people, which they presented in two volumes of *The Structure of Magic* (1975/76), developed into NLP and a bestselling book called *Frogs into Princes* (1979). The book is based on the transcripts of seminars conducted by Bandler and Grinder. The tone is informal, boundlessly confident, and challengingly iconoclastic:

> We call ourselves modelers. What we essentially do is to pay very little attention to what people say they do and a great deal of attention to what they do. And then we build ourselves a model of what they do. We are not psychologists, and we're also not theologians or theoreticians. We have no idea about the 'real' nature of things, and we're not particularly interested in what's 'true'. The function of modeling is to arrive at descriptions which are useful. So, if we happen to mention something that you know from a scientific study, or from statistics, is inaccurate, realize that a different level of experience is being offered you here. We're not offering you something that's true. Just things that are useful. (Bandler and Grinder 1979: 7)

Some of the principle ideas of NLP are not particularly controversial: that people are communicating all the time, and some of this is non-verbal; that the meaning of our communication is the response we get to it; that if what we do doesn't work, we should try doing something different; that we see the world through our own interpretations of it and those interpretations can change; and that we are inherently resourceful and the source of powerful qualities such as self-confidence, courage and compassion is within.

In *Frogs into Princes*, Bandler and Grinder demonstrate various methods for freeing people from dysfunctional responses and patterns of behaviour. They seem able to help people break old unconscious associations and establish new ones at remarkable speed. They describe this reprogramming as a Pavlovian process of stimulus–response conditioning, and it includes elements that might be called hypnosis. The key here is to create a kinesthetic anchor; to identify, in other words, a mental image or a gesture or a place that triggers a positive response and so creates a new thread of mental associations.

The other side of the same coin is called reframing. When you reframe something, 'what you are doing is attaching a new response to some sensory experience. You leave the content the same and put another piece of meaning around it' (Bandler and Grinder 1979: 7).

Outer games and quick fixes

Bandler and Grinder describe the process of anchoring as 'one of the most powerful covert tools you can use as a therapist or communicator'. This phrase points to a couple of aspects of NLP that make some critics uneasy. The sliding between therapist and communicator is troubling because it overlooks a crucial distinction: a therapist works on people with their knowledge and permission; a 'communicator', such as a salesperson or politician, does not. That blurring, coupled with the word 'covert', opens NLP to the charge of being underhand and manipulative. Even some self-professed fans of NLP have expressed reservations:

> The picture I have of the NLP 'industry' is one of something dynamic and positive but also tainted in places by perceptions of factionalism, ego-driven conflict, legal disputes and commercial greed. What is more, the rather grandiose-sounding claims made on behalf of NLP by some practitioners as something than can cure all phobias at a stroke and perform other 'miracles' do not seem to me to be reflected in daily experience or a significantly happier population. I know some of these cures work for some people some of the time but I rarely come across people who tell tales of NLP transforming their lives in a way it did mine. Even as a fan and practitioner myself I would certainly caution anyone against swallowing NLP uncritically. The key is to be able to identify those who work well and ethically with NLP – thankfully, they can be found. (Hayes 2008: 12)

The name itself seems to suggest that the process has some intellectual heft; that it's soundly rooted in neurology and linguistics. The third element suggests, at least subliminally, that a mind can be programmed as readily as a computer. The idea that the brain is like a computer was fashionable for a while, but turns out to be quite misleading. Computers have been made to replicate certain kinds of human activity. They have famously been able to beat humans at chess and, more recently, in general knowledge quizzes – impressive accomplishments. But these turn out to be quite computerish activities, involving an ability to sift at incredible speed through multiple options and databases. When it comes to questions, computers may be good at answering them, but the peculiarly human activity of coming up with original questions of their own is beyond their reach; as is experiencing an authentic emotion, or solving a problem, not by meticulously breaking it down into its component parts, but by grasping it whole in an inexplicable flash of insight. And this touches on what is essentially questionable about the NLP approach: that the detailed analysis and imitation of successful behaviour should be considered a route to behaving successfully.

In the NLP context, modelling sometimes refers to a way of creating rapport with a patient, or with a potential purchaser of NLP training. The process involves mirroring or pacing, to match your style to the style of the other person (Bandler and Grinder 1979: 79–80). But modelling also refers to this assumption, which lies at the root of NLP, that an imitation of externals can shape internal reality.

This emphasis on observation – what might be called the Outer Game of communication – reminds me of an exchange I once witnessed between a sociologist and a musician. The sociologist said, 'If Beethoven was such a great composer, why doesn't everyone just go on composing like Beethoven?' I thought the musician might say, 'Because some people prefer different kinds of music', or, 'Because Beethoven was a genius.' But his reply was more interesting: 'Because Beethoven wasn't composing like Beethoven. He was taking music from where it was and wrestling it towards some radically new place.'

It could equally be said that Virginia Satir was not practising therapy like Virginia Satir. A shift in posture that stems from an instinct for creating rapport means something different from the conscious imitation of that movement, however accurate the imitation, because human behaviour is an expression, not a performance, just as Beethoven's music is a journey, not a destination.

Implications for coaching

1. Being a coach requires us to take responsibility for ourselves and our actions and to repair or (to use an *est* term) complete the relationships in our lives. We can encourage our clients to do the same.
2. In the language of *est* and Landmark, a 'racket' is the habit of blaming someone else for something we perceive to be wrong in our lives. It can be a useful concept to discuss with your clients.
3. Another *est* process is clarifying the distinction between what happened to you and the 'story' you've created around it: *I lost my job, therefore I'm a loser.* This distinction is always worth exploring.
4. Mirroring the client's posture, breathing and energy level can be a powerful tool in creating rapport.
5. Be alert to the language your client uses, and to the assumptions contained within it that might be shaping and limiting her sense of reality. Encourage her to consider what other realities are possible.

Chapter 5: From tennis court to executive office: The Inner Game and GROW

The principles Tim Gallwey laid out in his first book not only underpin my coaching techniques but also provide sound advice for coping with life in general. One statement in particular stands out for me: *'In sports, I had to learn how to teach less so that more could be learned.'* This is something it took me years to truly understand as a coach. I gradually put away my enthusiasm for displaying my shiny toolkit, stopped thinking about my next 'brilliant' question, and simply concentrated so that my clients could follow the unique pathways of their own thoughts.

Sometimes the coach's question, however insightful, serves as a welcome distraction, enabling the client to veer away from the effort and agony of reaching the centre of the issue and taking a good hard look at it. While accepting that reflected words, prompting questions and other coaching interventions have their uses from time to time, I have come to appreciate the power of creating that space where, to paraphrase Gallwey, I am coaching less, so that more can be learned by my clients.

Carol Wilson
London, United Kingdom
carolwilson@performancecoachtraining.com
Managing Director: http://www.performancecoachtraining.com
Global Advisory Panellist: http://www.associationforcoaching.com

Timothy Gallwey and a new approach to coaching

Timothy Gallwey didn't invent sports psychology. That field has a history going back to the 1890s in America. In 1921 researchers were analysing Babe Ruth's swing and measuring his reaction time. By 1920 Germany had a specialized College of Physical Education, whose founder, Robert Werner Schulte, wrote a book called *Body and Mind in Sport*. The universities of Moscow and Leningrad had departments of sports psychology by the 1930s.

Coleman Griffith, who as professor of educational psychology at the University of Illinois had written about *The Psychology of Coaching* (1926) and

The Psychology of Athletics (1928), was working in the late 1930s for the Chicago Cubs, exploring the role of psychological and social factors in competitive performance (http://en.wikipedia.org/wiki/Sport_psychology 6 March 2012).

When Timothy Gallwey's *The Inner Game of Tennis* was published in 1974, there was plenty of advice available. But it was characteristically aimed at high-performing athletes. It was firmly rooted in a Western mindset that emphasized the competitive drive; and it still tended to be dominated by quantitative, laboratory-based analysis. As late as 1979, Illinois psychologist Rainer Martens was urging researchers to get out of the lab and into the field, to understand the real conditions under which athletes had to perform.

Gallwey not only took sports psychology onto the field of play, he made it relevant to players of any ability, and went on to draw a link between the ability to hit a ball with a racket and a whole range of other human activities. He had various things going for him: he combined his experience as a high-achieving athlete with a genuine interest in the struggles of players of no discernible talent. He had studied meditation techniques and was able to bring a significantly different perspective to the problem. And he could write. At Harvard, he'd not only captained the tennis team; he'd majored in English. Here is his description of the 'games people play'. The paragraph is worth quoting in full:

> That something else besides tennis is being played on the courts is obvious to the most casual observer. Regardless of whether he is watching the game at a country club, a public park or a private court, he will see players suffering everything from minor frustration to major exasperation. He will see the stomping of feet, shaking of fists, war dances, rituals, pleas, oaths and prayers; rackets are thrown against fences in anger, into the air for joy, or pounded against the concrete in disgust. Balls that are in will be called out, and vice versa. Linesmen are threatened, ball boys scolded and the integrity of friends questioned. On the faces of players you may observe, in quick succession, shame, pride, ecstasy and despair. Smug complacency gives way to high anxiety, cockiness to hangdog disappointment. Anger and aggression of varying intensity are expressed both openly and in disguised forms. If an observer was watching the game for the first time, it would be hard for him to believe that all this drama could be contained on a mere tennis court, between love-all and game, set and match. (Gallwey 1986: 94)

The power of The Inner Game

The essence of the problem, in Gallwey's view, is that in addition to the outer game – the competition with an external opponent and against external obstacles – there's an inner game, and to achieve success it's the inner game the player must first master: 'the player of The Inner Game comes to value the art of relaxed concentration above all other skills; he discovers a true basis for self-confidence; and he learns that the secret to winning any game lies in not trying too hard' (1986: 11). As Gallwey expresses it elsewhere, 'Only when the mind is still is one's peak performance reached' (1986: 22). There is a direct link here to a thread of mystical wisdom expressed in Eliot's prayer-like poem *Ash Wednesday*: 'Teach us to care and not to care/ Teach us to sit still' (Eliot 1964: 93) – to care, certainly, if our goal is to play better tennis, but not to get caught up in the distracting drama of our ball-by-ball performance. In a word familiar to students of Buddhism, Gallwey encourages us to avoid 'attachment'.

From his own experience as a tennis coach, he was all too aware of how an overload of instruction could clutter the mind of the student and achieve nothing but a disabling level of self-consciousness. 'Many students,' he writes, 'are too stroke-conscious and not attentive enough to results. Such players are aware of how they stroke the ball, but unconcerned with where it is actually going. It is often helpful for these players to shift their attention from means to ends' (Gallwey 1986: 47).

The calculations required to get the body in the right place and the racket moving at the right angle to make contact with a ball moving towards it at speed couldn't possibly be achieved in time by any cognitive process. All this must be left to one's inner intelligence. The role of the ego-mind is to provide information and feedback without judgement or criticism, to observe with maximum awareness, by watching, feeling and listening. Other than that, it must get out of the way.

In a memorable display of confidence in his own method, Gallwey gave a demonstration on camera for *60 Minutes*, an American current affairs programme. This piece of film brought Gallwey's ideas to a mass audience. On some viewers it had a huge and lasting impact. This comment was posted on Hacker News by a contributor using the name Sabat as recently as 2010:

> I saw a clip from *60 Minutes* in college that showed Tim Gallwey teaching tennis to a group of middle-aged people. None had ever played tennis before. He picked the person who showed the least potential and within 20 minutes had her serving better than I've ever served in my life. It made a huge impression on me. The book isn't really about tennis; it's how the human mind is meant to think and learn, and how far off we are in our preconceptions about those things.
> (Posted by SABAT on a site called Hacker News: http://news.ycombinator.com/item?id=1435759 6 March 2012)

The Inner Game goes into business

The Inner Game of Tennis was an immediate success and Gallwey went on to apply the same principles not only to other sports but to performance in the business world. According to Gallwey, at the heart of The Inner Game methodology are three principles, which have become foundational for coaching practice: 1) Non-judgemental awareness; 2) Trust in one's own self; and 3) The exercise of free and conscious choice (Gallwey 2009: xvii).

It's an unexpected leap, perhaps, to imagine this approach working for a business executive. It might seem counter-intuitive to take a physical skill involving coordination of hand and eye, a matching of the body's rhythm to the flight of the ball through the air, where the body must be allowed to respond instinctively without the distraction of the mind's nagging judgements, and to apply insights learned here to the multifaceted performance of someone managing a team or making business decisions. And yet the leap was clearly successful. Whatever the application, *The Inner Game* involves letting go of the ego and conscious striving, and balancing inner awareness with outer behaviour: 'What is needed is not so much the effort to improve ourselves, as the effort to become more aware of the beauty of what we already are' (Gallwey 1986: 122). In this sense, tennis was always a metaphor for more profound issues, and *The Inner Game* has as much in common with *Zen and the Art of Motorcycle Maintenance* (1974) as it has with mainstream sports psychology.

Gallwey's book on tennis appeared when developments in humanistic psychology, with their more optimistic models of human nature, were becoming established in the public consciousness. *The Inner Game* concept played a huge role in the early progress of life coaching and coaching in business and other professional fields, helping people to believe in themselves and trust their intuitive abilities.

Sir John Whitmore: a man for his time

In its unexpected turns, Sir John Whitmore's story could be seen as emblematic of the sixties. His father, Sir Francis Whitmore, had had a highly distinguished military career, serving as an officer in the Imperial Yeomanry in the Boer War. During the First World War he rose to the rank of Lieutenant-Colonel and commanded the 10th Royal Hussars. Four times he was mentioned in dispatches (an official record of courageous action), before being awarded the Distinguished Service Order. He was later appointed High Sheriff of Essex and Lord Lieutenant of Essex, and was created a Baronet in 1954.

John, who would later inherit his father's title, went to Eton, as his father had done, and trained at Sandhurst for a military career. In his twenties, however, his life journey became strikingly less predictable. He became a racing driver, achieving early success in the British Saloon Car Championship, but he discovered he was looking for something else, something more:

> After I'd done sports racing, I had this need to look inside rather than outside. I knew that's where the true richness was. I knew this was very important, despite the concerns of my parents. (Personal interview, 24 August 2011)

In 1969 he left England for California and spent time at the Esalen Institute. Inspired by what he found there, Whitmore returned with a film crew and was able to capture some powerful footage that would introduce the encounter group to a much wider audience (Chapter 2). One of the achievements of coaching, in whose development Whitmore would play a role, would be to take elements of talk therapy and the encounter process and fully democratize them, making the client an informed, consensual and equal partner in the engagement.

Intrigued by the problem of how to get the best out of people, Whitmore sought out Tim Gallwey, who had already published *The Inner Game of Tennis*. 'I met him in Malibu, California. We connected over sports. I wanted Tim to train me, and at first he was reluctant. In the end, the main reason he trained me was because I was English and he believed I could take *The Inner Game* to England' (Personal interview, 24 August 2011). There were cultural and economic differences between the two countries and, at first, coaching in Britain took a different route:

> Laura Whitworth was working on the West coast [of America] and Tom Leonard on the East. Initially, they were both looking at life coaching. Historically, people had much more expendable income in the US. People in England didn't have the money to pay for a personal coach. I was interested in the new application of the psychology of sport. I thought, I wonder if we can move this into business. We were running tennis programmes, and an executive at IBM was a keen tennis fan. He invited us into IBM. So we began teaching managers how to manage in a coaching fashion. We had corporate coaching on a collective basis before America. Coaching in Europe and America came up together but with different emphases – personal coaching in America and Executive and corporate coaching in England. (Personal interview, 24 August 2011)

The GROW model revisited

Whitmore was associated with a model which became highly successful in business coaching in the early years. The GROW model incorporates some of Gallwey's principles in a clear, straightforward formulation, identifying four steps: Goal (for the session as well as for the short and long term); Reality (checking to explore the current situation); Options (including alternative strategies or courses of action); and finally What is to be done, When and by Whom.

In retrospect, the success of the GROW model is not surprising. It captures, in a way that's easy to remember, a sequence that seems instinctively right. There are interesting parallels with research being conducted during the same period by academic psychologists David Kolb and Ron Fry, whose Experiential Learning Model identifies a cyclical pattern of four steps: concrete experience; observation of, and reflection on that experience; formation of abstract concepts based upon the reflection; and testing the new concepts. GROW encapsulated, in a happily appropriate acronym, some key elements in the decision-making process. The term was embedded in the subtitle of Whitmore's influential *Coaching for Performance: GROWing People, Performance and Purpose*, published in 1992. But in the text, Whitmore is insistent that 'GROW, without the context of AWARENESS and RESPONSIBILITY and the skill of questioning to generate them, has little value.' He remains uncomfortable with the simplistic uses to which the GROW model might be put.

> I'm not very happy with it . . . in 1991 when I wrote my book, I put it in there . . . and for that reason, it was attributed to me. But actually it's a problem because it doesn't really say anything about coaching. It's a model . . . yes, these things are important, you do need models to start with – as long as you don't think that this is the absolute truth. That's how religions started in the first place. (Personal interview, 24 August 2011)

The end of coaching

In the conclusion to *Coaching for Performance*, he repeats that there is 'no one right way to coach'. He not only foresees the danger of coaching ossifying into a formulaic system, he resists an attachment even to coaching itself as an activity independent of underlying principles that may be expressed in other ways:

> We may drop the word coaching or add new terms to the crop that already exist: counselling, facilitating, empowering, mentoring, supporting, guiding, psychotherapy. Their applications differ somewhat but they overlap, and though they may be expressed differently, the underlying principles of awareness, responsibility and self-belief are common to all. These principles are at the very core of human growth and effectiveness. (J. Whitmore 2004: 171)

He uses the final paragraphs of his book to propose a radical agenda, based on the belief that business 'feeds off and appeals to our lower nature, power and greed, but at the same time can be a vehicle for our creativity, aspiration and the will to good', arguing that coaching has a role in transforming business to bring it into alignment with 'higher and more caring human values' (J. Whitmore 2004: 172).

Now in his mid-seventies, Whitmore remains as idealistic as ever:

> That stuff in the sixties, Esalen and the anti-Vietnam war movement, were the first seeds of what is continuing today in human evolution . . . Finally we are coming to a point where people will take responsibility for themselves and not rely on a hierarchy . . . The primary product of coaching is self-responsibility. Coaching grew up to meet this need. We've got to get to the stage of self-responsibility for everyone. When that happens, the word coaching will disappear. (Personal interview, 24 August 2011)

These are profound words from one of the elders of our profession. As coaches, we are engaged in the business not just of helping people to enjoy more fulfilling lives, but also of encouraging them to take responsibility.

Implications for coaching

1. Gallwey's three principles include non-judgemental awareness; trust in one's own self; and the exercise of free and conscious choice. These are core values for us as coaches, and can be very helpful to our clients.
2. Help your client to keep her eyes on the prize – to think about what she intends to achieve – and hold that desired *end* in mind as a source of motivation, when she finds herself overwhelmed by the detailed complexity of *means*.
3. Whitmore's GROW model is easy to work with and can give your coaching structure and purpose. Start by helping the client to frame a goal, to which you can return during the engagement, to check progress and to make modifications if necessary.
4. Encourage your client to be clear about the reality stage of the GROW model. Ask questions such as 'What is happening at the moment?', 'How important is this to you?' and 'What impact is this having on you?'
5. A helpful component of the GROW methodology involves asking scaling questions to allow the client to assess progress. For example: 'Where are you now on a scale of 1 to 10?'

Part 2
What makes us tick

Chaos of thought and passion, all confused;
Still by himself abused or disabused;
Created half to rise and half to fall;
Great lord of all things, yet a prey to all,
Sole judge of truth, in endless error hurled;
The glory, jest and riddle of the world.

Alexander Pope: *Essay on Man*

Man is many things, but he is not rational.

Oscar Wilde: *The Picture of Dorian Gray*

Chapter 6: Tapping the unconscious: Sigmund Freud and Carl Jung

The psychodynamic paradigm brings to coaching the perspective of the unconscious psychological processes of the human being and the underlying dynamics being played out in relationships. Specifically, I find very useful the concept of defence mechanisms (for example, denial, intellectualization, substitution, compensation, rationalization, projection). In difficult situations in corporate life, employees' coping strategies often result in feelings of discomfort, tension, stress, threat and pain. These are common among executives, though most of the time ignored or denied. So when my coachee rationalizes away the results of a 360° interview, I point out that this might be a sign that he is struggling to protect himself from a painful realization or feeling. Also when my coachee shares a strong reaction to a behaviour or attitude of another, judging the person severely, it may be that he is projecting his own undesirable feelings onto that person.

Psychodynamic theory helps me understand what emotions and feelings come from me and what belongs to my coachee. In fact, by being aware of my own issues, triggers, 'hot buttons' and preconceptions, I am able to support the coachee's awareness of his covert feelings, beliefs, needs, motivations. These affect the way he behaves and, therefore, the dynamics he helps create, which define the role he plays at work.

The psychodynamic process of transference occurs when the coachee unconsciously sees the coach through the lens of a significant person from his past; and counter-transference, when the coach responds. Parallel process is another helpful tool. It occurs when the coaching relationship reveals the way the coachee functions in other relationships. All of these psychodynamic tools are useful, and ultimately contribute to support my coachee's growth.

Ana Oliveira Pinto
Executive Development Consultant and Coach
Lisbon, Portugal
a.c.oliveirapinto@gmail.com

Sigmund Freud: moulder of thought

I was born in America in the mid-twentieth century, when the reputation of Sigmund Freud (1856–1939) was probably at its peak. It's taken a lot of knocks since then. When I was growing up, psychoanalysis was an expensive indulgence for the few, but the role of the analyst had a cultural status that commanded respect. In a book on Freud and his successors, published in 1961, the British psychiatrist J. A. C. Brown observed that among the general public, 'the psychoanalyst reigns supreme and psychology and psychiatry are seen either as synonyms for or as rather insignificant ramifications of Freudian theory.' (Brown 1987: 37)

Brown placed Freud in the same league as Copernicus and Darwin. Of those earlier scientists, Copernicus who transformed the map of our local part of the universe by shifting the earth from the still centre to hurl it into orbit around the sun, and Darwin who placed humankind on the same family tree as the rest of the animal kingdom, Brown said this:

> inadequate, unsound or downright wrong as some of their reasons may have been, we have regarded the world in a totally different light since we discovered our insignificant position in relation to the rest of the universe and our biological continuity with other living things, and it is not unreasonable to suggest that the transformation was completed by Freud, whose work implied that man's godlike intellect was, as H. G. Wells expressed it, 'no more designed for discovering the truth than a pig's snout'. (Brown 1987: 2)

In Brown's view, Freud was up there with the greatest thinkers in the history of science; and not just one of a series, but the last of them, the one who brought the process to completion. It's a bold claim. But even while making it, Brown finds it necessary to acknowledge that Freud didn't get everything right, and he does it by conceding unspecified weaknesses in the *reasoning* of Copernicus and Darwin, which was – like Freud's, he implies – sometimes 'inadequate, unsound or downright wrong'. Brown goes on to say that, in common with these earlier scientists, Freud was 'a moulder of thought rather than a mere discoverer of facts' (Brown 1987: 2). The casual disparaging of facts implied in that phrase reveals a defensive attitude to Freud's achievement.

The defensiveness is understandable. The reputations of both Copernicus and Darwin depend on facts that can be simply stated. The earth is in orbit around the sun, not the other way round, and humans, rather than being created whole and complete a few thousand years ago, evolved by natural selection, as did every other species on the planet: the earth is in motion, and gorillas are our evolutionary cousins. What Freud discovered is harder to pin down. So much of what he taught in detail about the human psyche is now discredited. And yet his name remains firmly attached to a way of looking at human experience that seems to set us apart from our pre-Freudian ancestors. Where to place Freud and how to assess him is complicated by the fact that he still has the power to cause controversy.

Freud under attack

Freud had never been without opponents, and at the start of the 1960s, when Brown's book was published, he was about to acquire some new ones. Ken Kesey's 1962 novel, *One Flew Over the Cuckoo's Nest*, presented the inmates of a mental ward as victims of oppression and coercion. Its target is, in fact, an un-Freudian system of treatment which includes drugs, electroconvulsive therapy, and a manipulative regime of rewards and shame. But the book was in tune with the decade's anti-establishment mood and typified a growing resistance to conformity of all kinds, including submission to the authority of mental health professionals. The Scottish psychiatrist R. D. Laing, who entertained the possibility that madness might be a sane response to an insane predicament, worked to break down professional hierarchies by having therapists and patients living communally. An anti-psychiatry movement should perhaps have boosted the cause of Freud's talking cure, but the austere discipline of the psychoanalytic couch was beginning to seem archaic with the development of more experimental and openly confrontational forms of therapy.

The 1960s saw the rise of the New Left, who followed the old Left in attending to external causes of distress, such as material deprivation, discrimination, and political disempowerment, and was inclined to see the narrow focus on individual neurosis as a costly and frivolous distraction. Meanwhile, those seeking spiritual insight and attracted to eastern mysticism were discovering Freud's most famous ex-disciple, Carl Jung. For Freud, religious belief was a form of neurosis, and altruism a sublimated expression of the sexual instinct. Jung saw higher possibilities for the human spirit, and as Jung's stock rose, Freud's fell.

Soon enough there would be the women's movement, with its own reasons to dislike Freud, starting with the concept of penis envy. Although Freud's most famous early patients were female, his theories of childhood sexuality focused on the male experience, and were extended to females sometimes only as an afterthought. According to Freud, the young boy goes through an oedipal phase during which he harbours sexual feelings towards his mother and feelings of aggression towards his father. Fearing that he will be punished by his father with castration, he gives up hope of fulfilling his desires and forms an alliance with his father. This transition enables him to form a satisfactory male identity. But what if the child is female? Noticing the absence of a penis, she concludes that she has already received the punishment of castration, for which she holds her mother responsible. She turns her affection towards her father, fantasizing that he will make her pregnant. The baby will compensate her for not having a penis.

In rebelling against a whole range of patriarchal assumptions, feminists saw Freud as a legitimate target of their outrage or mockery. Gloria Steinem famously remarked that sending a woman to a Freudian therapist is not so far distant from sending a Jew to a Nazi. The feminist critique of Freud has made it difficult, if not impossible, for anyone to defend the concept of penis envy without backtracking considerably from Freud's position. In an invaluable introduction to Freud, Anthony Storr offers this thoughtful explanation:

> In Freud's era, male dominance was even more evident than it is today. Because men hold most of the power, many women consider themselves inferior, unappreciated, despised, or weak. Producing babies is one way in which women can feel superior or equal to men. If we express Freud's idea in psychological, rather than anatomical, terms, very few people would take issue with it. (Storr 1989: 35)

This sounds very reasonable, but Freud saw human behaviour as rooted in our basic biological condition, not in variable factors of culture and society; and there's no indication that the concepts of penis envy and castration anxiety were meant only as metaphors. It would be interesting to imagine an equivalent defence of Copernicus or Darwin. The earth revolves around the sun only in the sense that we feel it to be central to our existence? We're related to chimpanzees only in the sense that we share the experience of living on the earth? No such defence is imaginable, because it isn't necessary.

Memories, fantasies and inventions

Freud's ideas evolved during his working life, and his belief that children have sexual fantasies about their parents was not the first position he adopted. In a paper written in 1896 he had taken a very different line, asserting that hysterical symptoms can always be traced back to premature sexual experience. (Freud was already 40, but had only recently begun publishing on psychoanalysis.) It was not until a few years later that he decided that experiences reported to him in therapy were memories of childhood fantasies, not of real events. It was a momentous shift, which drove the focus of his treatment deeper into the hidden world of the individual psyche.

Some people have argued that Freud changed his mind so as not to cause offence to bourgeois Viennese society. Given how persistently offensive Freud's ideas continued to be, however, this seems an unlikely motive. More probably he genuinely recoiled from the sheer improbability of so much child abuse.

Who can say now whether the reported experiences had really happened, had been imagined in childhood, or were being served up to order by suggestible patients eager to please their therapist? Whatever the historical truth, this development in Freud's thinking would be subjected to fresh scrutiny in the 1980s, when adult victims of child abuse began to speak more openly about their experiences and we all had to wake up to the distressing fact that abuse was more widespread that we had imagined. Freud's retreat came to appear emblematic of the kind of denial and disbelief that victims of abuse had traditionally encountered, and the direct cause of it for those who had found themselves analysed into silence by orthodox psychoanalysts.

The late 1980s and 1990s brought a fresh reason to haul Freud over the coals, this time from the other side of the same issue. In *Unauthorised Freud: Doubters Confront a Legend* Frederick C. Crews drew together essays and extracts from 18 authors to build the case against psychoanalysis. For Crews, this cause was given fresh urgency by the 'so-called recovered memory movement, which has been causing incalculable personal, familial, and social havoc'. Crews continues:

> The emergence of latter-day psychoanalytic incest inquisitors constitutes the most dramatic sign that the work of this present book is neither antiquarian nor superfluous but urgently practical. As I have shown elsewhere, every feature of recovered memory therapy, even the crudest, was pioneered by Freud . . . Moreover, the recovered memory movement would have been inconceivable without our society's more diffuse allegiance to the Freudian psychodynamic paradigm. (Crews 1998: xi)

No one was more closely associated than Freud with the idea that a memory could be stored out of sight to be unpacked years later fresh and whole, untainted by the expectations of the therapist doing the unpacking. For some, such as Crews, this controversial application of an essentially Freudian idea had the effect of testing the analytical method to destruction. This controversy brought the Freudian concept of the repressed memory up against research that has revealed how fluid memories can be, how dependent they are on the process of telling and re-telling, and how easy to is to plant false memories by suggestion.

Freud's legacy

I review this history not to debunk Freud, but to reflect on the scope and intensity of the attacks on his ideas during my lifetime and to observe that, in spite of it all, Freud is still a force to be reckoned with. After much has been discarded, much remains to enlighten us about our own motivation and the motivation of all the other people we deal with. Freud taught us the extent to which we are all actors performing in plays of our own making. I may be under the illusion that I am an autonomous adult interacting with other autonomous adults, but at any moment, a primal relationship with a parent or a sibling will superimpose itself on the conversation. We all carry internal representations of the world in inaccessible regions of the mind and project elements of it onto partners and colleagues. We marry versions of our mothers or our fathers in repeated attempts to work through unresolved conflicts. We play roles in our personal and professional relationships that were laid down in infancy. We engage in a variety of strategies, such as denial and rationalization, to protect ourselves from uncomfortable truths. We reveal our unconscious feelings in verbal slips and we sabotage our conscious purposes by forgetting appointments and missing trains. We know what it means to be accident-prone or passive-aggressive. So much of what we now know, or half know, or take for granted about the complexity of human interaction derives from Freud. We have adopted and internalized so many terms of Freudian origin that Freud has entered our bloodstream.

Even technical terms specific to the psychoanalytical process have seeped out of the consulting room to achieve wider currency; *transference*, for example, the specific form of projection that Freud detected when his patients expressed feelings of attraction or dependence, and which he considered both a nuisance and a therapeutic tool, since it seemed to bring old familial relationships into the room for closer examination.

Freud and the unconscious

The hostility that Freud encountered in his own time, and which his ideas continue to evoke, is part of the point. He had a talent for getting under people's skin. He presented an unflattering image of the mind that profoundly unsettled any common sense assumption that we can truly know ourselves or take charge of our lives. Thinking about Freud's impact, 20 years after his death, Carl Jung spoke about Freud's relentlessly confrontational style:

> Like an Old Testament prophet, he undertook to overthrow false gods, to rip the veils away from a mass of dishonesties and hypocrisies, mercilessly exposing the rottenness of the contemporary psyche. He did not falter in the face of the unpopularity such an enterprise entailed. The impetus which he gave to our civilization sprang from his discovery of an avenue to the unconscious. By evaluating dreams as the most important source of information concerning the unconscious processes, he gave back to mankind a tool that had seemed irretrievably lost. (Jung 1965: 169)

Here Jung identifies Freud's work on dreams as Freud's great achievement. *The Interpretation of Dreams*, which was the book that made Freud's name, was published in 1899. Jung read it for the first time the following year when he was 25 years old and had just begun working as a psychiatrist in Zurich. What rang true for Jung in Freud's dream theory was that dreams reveal material that the conscious mind has repressed. In general that's an idea we're all familiar with, and put in those terms it doesn't sound particularly controversial. But Freud's explanation of the way dreams work is actually quite counter-intuitive.

Freud had begun with the idea of a simple division between the conscious and the unconscious parts of the mind. What was repressed resided in the unconscious. But this led him to wonder what agency governed the process of repression. Which part of the mind was it that policed the unconscious, keeping its powerful impulses hidden? Freud concluded that there was a third agency. So he came to see the mind divided in three parts: the id, the ego and the super-ego.

The mind of the new born is nothing but id. This region of the mind is primitive, emotional, anarchic. It has no organized purpose except to satisfy instinctive needs. Essentially what drives the id is the sexual instinct. As the child grows and submits to the authority of parents and the wider society, the voices of parental reproof and control are internalized in the super-ego. The super-ego observes and monitors the self, serving as conscience and critic. Struggling between these is the ego, pulled one way by powerful impulses whose sources are buried too deep for scrutiny, pulled the other way by demands too familiar to be questioned and, as if all that wasn't enough, having to respond to external reality. Not surprisingly, the main role of the ego is self-preservation.

Dreams arise from the id. Most dreams are wish fulfilments and express sexual wishes repressed since infancy. The true meaning of the dream – what Freud called its *latent* content – would be too disturbing to the ego in its raw form. The role of the super-ego is to protect the ego by disguising the dream's meaning. This disguised version, the dream's *manifest* content, is what the dreamer remembers on waking. The dream is made incoherent and fragmentary to hide its significance. Any narrative element, far from offering a clue as to the dream's meaning, is a further layer of obfuscation. The role of the therapist is to help the patient to unscramble the dream, to decode what the super-ego has encrypted. This is achieved by free association. Any detail in the dream can serve as a starting point for a sequence of associations that must lead eventually to the dream's meaning.

We now know that infants dream. Even foetuses dream after the 28th week. So dreams are not dependent on the division of the ego from the id and occur long before any impulses have been repressed.

Carl Jung: disillusioned disciple

Eventually, for different reasons, Carl Jung (1875–1961) took issue with these basic aspects of Freud's theory. For one thing, he challenged Freud on the nature of what we repress from our conscious minds.

> [Freud] considered the cause of the repression to be a sexual trauma. From my practice, however, I was familiar with numerous cases of neurosis in which the question of sexuality played a subordinate part, other factors standing in the foreground – for example, the problem of social adaptation, of oppression by tragic circumstances of life, prestige considerations, and so on. Later I presented such cases to Freud; but he would not grant that factors other than sexuality could be the cause. (Jung 1965: 147)

One way of looking at this disagreement is to consider that Freud and Jung were both right, but they were looking at different levels of reality. In the spirit of the kind of scientific enquiry that aims to reduce things to their component parts, Freud was attempting to strip human motivation to its most basic level. Later in the twentieth century, natural scientists would become fascinated by ecological systems and the intricately organized patterns that emerge from apparently chaotic data. But in Freud's time, the most exciting developments were in nuclear physics. The electron had been discovered in 1897. While Freud was writing *The Interpretation of Dreams*, scientists were identifying the different kinds of radiation emanating from atoms. Rightly or wrongly Freud considered himself a scientist. He wasn't interested in the diversity of human feeling or the variety of social interaction. If we are organisms whose first function is to reproduce, it follows that a man's concern with 'prestige' is merely a manifestation of an unresolved castration anxiety or, more generally, a biological need to compete sexually. This is an area of Freudian thinking that has entered the popular consciousness, and has proved useful in putting masculine competitiveness in perspective. Feminist anti-nuclear protestors in the 1980s chanting, *We don't care how big your missile is*, were channelling Freud. But for the individual patient (or coaching client) struggling with 'prestige considerations', it would perhaps be more helpful, as well as showing more respect, to follow Jung's lead: pay attention to the patient's concerns by exploring what prestige means to him and how he might either achieve more of it or liberate himself from its demands.

In analysing dreams, Jung was less interested than Freud in identifying phallic symbols and suchlike. He considered such one-to-one correspondences of limited value. What Freud called a symbol was, for Jung, merely a sign, a simple substitution of one thing for another. A true symbol is harder to translate because it's directing us towards something we don't already know, an intuitive idea that the unconscious is striving to communicate. As in literature, symbols in dreams are not designed to obscure meaning but to reveal it:

> I was never able to agree with Freud that the dream is a 'façade' behind which its meaning lies hidden – a meaning already known but maliciously, so to speak, withheld from consciousness. To me dreams are a part of nature, which harbors no intention to deceive, but expresses something as best it can, just as a plant grows or an animal seeks its food as best it can. (Jung 1965: 163)

The images of growth and nourishment are significant. For Jung, communications from the unconscious serve the purpose of helping us reconcile conflicts in our present reality and lead us forward to the next stage of our continuing development. In *Memories, Dreams, Reflections*, Jung describes one particular dream that was of great significance in the development of his thinking and in widening the gulf between his vision and Freud's.

In the dream, Jung found himself in a beautifully furnished upstairs room. Realizing that this unfamiliar house was his, he went downstairs to explore the ground floor. Here everything was darker, with medieval furnishings. Descending a stone stairway to the cellar he found a vaulted room that dated from Roman times. Discovering a stone slab in the floor with a ring in it, he lifted the slab and went down into a room cut out of the rock. In the dust on the floor were fragments of pottery, bones and two human skulls.

In Freud's view, the dream revealed a death wish. Jung, on the other, felt that he had been given an image of the psyche. The inhabited space of the upstairs room represented consciousness; the ground floor, the first level of the unconscious: 'The deeper I went, the more alien and the darker the scene became. In the cave, I discovered remains of a primitive culture, that is, the world of the primitive man within myself – a world which can scarcely be reached or illuminated by consciousness' (Jung 1965: 160).

The collective unconscious

For Jung, this dream was the first intimation of what he would later call the collective unconscious, the idea of a deeply buried part of the psyche that contains an inherited memory, and out of which arise archetypal images. For Jung, these archetypes provide, among other things, an instinctive understanding of what life demands of us at different stages. We are programmed at a deep level to fulfil a variety of functions: to learn language, for example, to acquire the values of our community, to be initiated into adulthood, to raise children, to be providers, to take on the responsibilities of maturity. Stages such as these are present across cultures and throughout human history. Jung found them reflected in different mythological systems and embodied in all kinds of rituals. Modern urban life cuts us off from activities such as hunting and gathering on which our ancestors depended and alienates us in other ways from the mythical dimension of life. The challenge is to stay in touch with our creativity and to grow, in Jung's term, towards *individuation*.

Jung sometimes made a distinction between the archetype and the archetypal image. An archetype might be thought of in crude terms as a kind of universal template, though it's hard to know anything about it, in fact, because it's so deeply buried in the unconscious. The archetypal image is the form in which the archetype comes to us and is partly determined by culture. Those of our dreams that come from the collective unconscious tap into the same source of images as myths and folk tales.

Our sense of gender is shaped by innate images of masculinity and femininity. For each gender the contrasting archetypal image, the *anima* in men, the *animus* in women, is of profound imaginative power. Other archetypes help to guide us through life's stages. At each stage different needs make themselves felt, new impulses demand expression. Traditional rites of passage are designed to help people through critical transitions. Jung argued that in midlife we experience a shift from the biological and social needs associated with having children and providing for them, towards cultural and spiritual needs. He didn't use the term midlife crisis, but the concept shows his influence.

Between the collective unconscious and the ego lies the region Jung called the personal unconscious. This contains what has been repressed, as well as experiences that the ego has not fully registered or understood, and material that has been temporarily suppressed while the conscious mind directs its attention elsewhere.

The persona and the shadow

As we grow up we conform to adult expectations, pushing unacceptable tendencies out of sight. We learn to wear a mask, to adopt a *persona*. This is often suited to our occupation or, more broadly, to the role we play. It's necessary to develop a persona in order to integrate successfully into adult life, but it has drawbacks. It can trap us into a way of behaving that does not allow full expression to who we are. When people act out of character, they are showing the repressed part of themselves, what Jung calls the *shadow*. If I take an irrational dislike to somebody, it may be my own shadow that I'm recognizing and reacting against. Jung developed his views of the ego and its relationship to the personal unconscious in his theory of personality types.

My shadow is personal to me but, since it contains elements repressed since infancy, it shares instinctive impulses, such as aggression, lust and avarice, that are common to humankind. So it is connected to a collective shadow. The figures we demonize as a society, or the superstitious fears we create, emerge from the collective shadow. It's necessary for our mental health to learn to live with the shadow. Self-acceptance and self-forgiveness are necessary. The more deeply buried are our contrary impulses, the more likely they are to take us by surprise, sometimes with disastrous consequences. 'The unconscious therefore, in Jung's view, is not merely a cellar where man dumps his rubbish, but the source of consciousness and of the creative and destructive spirit of mankind' (Fordham 1964: 27–8).

Art and the spirit

To begin with, Jung was a disciple and loyal supporter of Freud. When they met for the first time in Vienna in 1907 they experienced a kind of mutual infatuation: by Jung's account, they spoke for 13 hours with hardly a pause. Jung was groomed to be Freud's successor. In 1911 he became the first president of the International Psychoanalytic Society. But the publication in 1912 of *The Psychology of the Unconscious*, in which Jung criticized Freud's theories, led the following year to an irrevocable rift. Jung found himself written off as a mystic. In Jung's view, 'Freud, who had always made much of his irreligiosity had now constructed a dogma' (Jung 1965: 151). In retrospect, he identified the question of spirituality as the greatest obstacle between them:

> Above all, Freud's attitude toward the spirit seemed to me highly questionable. Wherever, in a person or in a work of art, an expression of spirituality (in the intellectual, not the supernatural sense) came to light, he suspected it, and insinuated that it was repressed sexuality. Anything that could not be directly interpreted as sexuality he referred to as 'psychosexuality'. I protested that this hypothesis, carried to its logical conclusion, would lead to an annihilating judgment upon culture. Culture would then appear as a mere farce, the morbid consequence of repressed sexuality. 'Yes,' he assented, 'so it is, and that is just a curse of fate against which we are powerless to contend.' (Jung 1965: 149–50)

Freud tended to diminish artistic creation to the level of wish fulfilment, seeing it as merely a sublimated expression of unsatisfied sexual wishes. Strangely, for a man who devoted time to art and literature and seemed capable of appreciating them at a sophisticated level, Freud often writes about art as though it has no more value than childish play and fantasy. There is something suspect, and potentially neurotic, in a grown person devoting a life to artistic enterprises.

> An artist . . . is oppressed by excessively powerful instinctual needs. He desires to win honour, power, wealth, fame, and the love of women; but he lacks the means for achieving these satisfactions.

> Consequently, like any unsatisfied man, he turns away from reality
> and transfers all his interests, his libido too, to the wishful
> constructions of his life of phantasy, whence the path might lead to
> neurosis. (Freud, quoted in Storr 1989: 101)

In rejecting the reductive aspects of Freud's teaching, Jung departed also
from his therapeutic practice. He dispensed with the couch, favouring instead
two chairs facing each other. Rather than encouraging regression to a childhood state, he wanted to lead patients to a sense of adult responsibility.
He understood neurosis as the suffering of a soul that has not found its
meaning – as a response not to a memory of early trauma, but to the challenge
of a life event in the present. The key question for the therapist to bear in
mind, therefore, is not what event in infancy caused this condition, but *what
task is the patient trying to avoid?* 'The real therapy only begins when the patient
sees that it is no longer father and mother who are standing in his way, but
himself.' The therapist, too, must be present, meeting the patient as an equal
partner in the process; he must 'emerge from his anonymity and give an
account of himself, just as he expects his patients to do' (Jung, quoted in
Stevens 1994: 131).

From couch to coaching

If we look in this history for the seeds of coaching, we must recognize a
development in the 1890s when Freud abandoned hypnosis in treating
hysteria and began to experiment with free association, encouraging the
patient to speak spontaneously. This was a revolutionary moment, opening
up the medical consultation to a process of self-discovery and an exploration
of the patient's inner life.

Jung's rejection of the couch and what it symbolized was a step of
equivalent importance. According to the Jungian analyst Anthony Stevens,
'Many patients who consulted Jung have testified to the cordiality, warmth,
and courtesy with which they were received. His sense of humour, always in
evidence, made it impossible for him to seem pompous or self-important, and
he never attempted to disguise his own fallibility as a human being' (Stevens
1994: 126). In a fascinating passage in *Memories, Dreams, Reflections*, Jung
reflects on the feelings he experienced after leaving Freud's circle, and the
effect of that separation on his practice.

> After the parting of the ways with Freud, a period of inner uncertainty
> began for me. It would be no exaggeration to call it a state of
> disorientation. I felt totally suspended in mid-air, for I had not yet
> found my own footing. Above all, I found it necessary to develop a
> new attitude toward my patients. I resolved for the present not to

bring any theoretical premises to bear upon them, but to wait and see what they would tell of their own accord. My aim became to leave things to chance. The result was that patients would spontaneously report their dreams and fantasies to me, and I would merely ask, 'What occurs to you in connection with that?' or, 'How do you mean that, where does that come from, what do you think about it?' The interpretations seemed to follow of their own accord from the patients' replies and associations. (Jung 1965: 170)

In withdrawing any kind of ideology or any sense of expertise over the issues the patients presented, Jung became more personally present. In many ways, this paragraph reads like a blueprint for a coaching session.

Implications for coaching

As coaches, we don't practise psychotherapy, either of the Freudian or Jungian type. However, many of our assumptions about what we do when we work with clients have been influenced by these two thinkers.

1. As coaches, we don't dwell on a client's past. However, we need to remember that much of what determines a client's attitude, beliefs, and emotional make-up probably originated in childhood. References to the past should not be dismissed.
2. Dreams may be important clues to understanding the self. As coaches, we aren't in the business of dream analysis, but we can be aware of the impact of dreams on the human psyche.
3. Much of what people do and feel is not necessarily rational or conscious. Understanding psychodynamics can help coaches both comprehend and manage non-rational behaviours.
4. Resistance is often encountered in coaching sessions. Psychodynamics can help us understand that resistance is a normal reaction, and that we need to be prepared for this.
5. We should be alert to our own and our client's tendencies to project positive and negative feelings.

Chapter 7: Our bodies ourselves: from Wilhelm Reich to Julio Olalla

For me, it's inconceivable how we coaches can do our work effectively without including the body in our methodology and approach. After all, we human beings have bodies. Not only that, but the way we use them and incorporate them into our daily activities of living absolutely influences the results we get or don't get.

Let me give you an example. Anna was a mid-level manager in HR who, after being on the job for about nine months, was having difficulty getting buy-in to her ideas. At our first meeting, she was contracted and tight. She spoke quickly, made little eye contact and spoke, primarily, out of the mood of frustration. My hunch, based on her shape and presence, was that she was a 'bull-in-a-china-shop' and had no awareness of how she appeared to other people. I noticed my own reaction to her was to tense up and I had to do my own centring practice to get present and connected with her as she talked. So, after establishing trust and rapport, I asked for her permission to share my own somatic reaction to her and asked if she was aware of the effect she had on others. She was open to the idea, so we worked on reshaping her when she engaged with others so that she occurred more open, flexible, available and present to them. She took on a daily practice of this and reported two weeks later that her boss actually asked her what had happened because she seemed so much more relaxed around the office.

Without Anna becoming aware of her movements-in-action and their consequences, she was doomed to keep repeating the behaviours that weren't working. Her ideas were sound, but the body she delivered them in didn't generate the results she wanted – and that was where our coaching had the most leverage and impact.

Terrie Lupberger, Master Certified Coach
Boulder, Colorado, USA
terrie@terrielupberger.com
http://www.terrielupberger.com

Wilhelm Reich: controversial visionary

Wilhem Reich was an extraordinary, innovative radical therapist. But even his great admirer, Fritz Perls, thought that in his later years he had gone mad. His work became dominated by his obsession with the orgone accumulator. Orgone was Reich's own 'discovery', a kind of primordial energy running through the body, whose flow could be blocked by traumatic experiences. Freud had seen libidinal energy as one of two basic human impulses, the other being the aggressive impulse. Reich expanded this idea and literalized it, treating sexual energy as an essential and measurable force in the human body and, eventually, in nature generally. He invented the orgone accumulator, a metal container in which the patient would sit while this energy was captured and channelled. The general concept, if not this particular machine, would be parodied in Woody Allen's 1973 film *Sleeper*, in which Allen, waking up in the future, is put inside an orgasmatron.

Reich had been conducting experiments on these lines for some years, when a journalist called Mildred Brady wrote a piece for *The New Republic* entitled, 'The Strange Case of Wilhelm Reich'. Brady had been researching the Bohemian subculture of Big Sur, California, a place of startling natural beauty which was home, long before Esalen was conceived, to a community of artists and writers. 'The person they admired most of all, Mildred Brady reported, was Wilhelm Reich, the renegade psychiatrist who called the state a conspiracy against the healthy needs of the natural human body and the orgasm the supreme human experience' (Anderson 2004: 20).

The subheading of Brady's article on Reich, when *The New Republic* published it in 1947, mixed the explosive ingredients that would turn the material for an academic dispute into a scandal, and gave them a good shake: 'The man who blames both neurosis and cancer on unsatisfactory sexual activities has been repudiated by only one scientific journal.' It's all there – sex, cancer and the obtuseness of the academic elite, and, at the heart of the story, a dangerously wacky shrink. Did it make any difference that Reich was a German Jew? Perhaps not, but McCarthyism was already disproportionately targeting Jewish artists and intellectuals in its increasingly paranoid search for un-American activities. And Reich had previous form. In the wake of the bombing of Pearl Harbor he had been detained, and questioned on Ellis Island, as an immigrant with communist connections. Searching his home, the FBI had found a copy of both Hitler's *Mein Kampf* and Trotsky's autobiography.

He had, in fact, joined the communist party in Berlin in 1930, but unwilling to submit to party doctrines and discipline had been expelled in 1933. That same year he was attacked in the Nazi press for his book, *The Sexual Struggle of Youth*. The Nazis objected to him as a communist and an advocate of free love, prompting Reich to leave the country and seek safety elsewhere.

The following year it was the turn of Danish critics to accuse him of 'corrupting Danish youth with German sexology'.

It's hard to deny Reich's courage. Whether or not his orgone theory made any sense, and whatever we think of his emphasis on the orgasm in psychological healing, he was certainly willing to engage in these intellectual explorations in the face of hostile attacks and at risk of imprisonment. In the mid-1950s, his orgone accumulator was investigated by the US Food and Drug Administration. Unwilling to cooperate with the authorities, Reich was sentenced to two years in prison. He wrote, 'I would like to plead for my right to investigate natural phenomena without having guns pointed at me. I also ask for the right to be wrong without being hanged for it' (Sharaf 1994: 4–5). He died of heart failure before he was released.

Childhood dramas

The major events of Reich's childhood read like the plot for a gothic novel, or perhaps more aptly, a fictional treatment of a character in urgent need of Freudian analysis. This reference to Freud is not meant frivolously. Accounts of Reich's early life depend on his own testimony, which is perhaps inevitably filtered through Freudian preoccupations, such as infantile sexuality, incest fantasies and patricidal urges.

Wilhelm Reich (1897–1957) was brought up in Bukovina, an area on the border of Romania and Ukraine, but then part of the Austro-Hungarian Empire. His father, a prosperous cattle farmer, was an assimilated Jew who was proud of his German culture and would not allow the young Wilhelm to play with Yiddish-speaking children (Sharaf 1994: 39). The parents seem to have played conventional roles – the father authoritarian and violent, the mother gentle and affectionate. Reich gave inconsistent accounts of his early sexual experiences, but he was apparently sexually precocious. At an early age he observed the coachman having sex with the housemaid and made various attempts to imitate this behaviour, both with the maid herself and with his younger brother's nurse. According to his memoir *Passion of Youth*, he lost his virginity at the age of 11 with the cook, though elsewhere he said he was 13.

Until he was 10, he was tutored at home and had plenty of opportunity to get drawn into the family drama, which was not in short supply. His mother was having an affair with one of his tutors and he would follow her to the tutor's bedroom and listen at the door with confused feelings. There are different accounts of what happened next. Perhaps, in retribution for her failure to protect him from his beatings, he shopped her to his father. Perhaps he only thought about doing this. Either way, his father found out, for which Wilhelm blamed himself. His mother made a number of attempts at suicide, finally killing herself when Wilhelm was 14. His father died three years later, possibly as a result of deliberately inducing pneumonia by exposing himself to the cold (Sharaf 1994).

War, sex and communism

In 1915, when Reich was 18, the Russians invaded Bukovina and Reich and his brother escaped to Vienna, abandoning their home and possessions. He joined the Austro-Hungarian Army and served for three years. When the war was over he went to medical school in Vienna where he studied with Freud, showing exceptional talent. By the age of 23, while still an undergraduate, he was a regular member of the Vienna Psychoanalytic Association and was seeing patients for analysis under Freud's supervision. At 25 he married Annie Fink, a 20-year-old student who was seeing him for analysis. They moved to Berlin where, while practising as a Freudian psychoanalyst, he taught sex education, wrote his book *The Sexual Revolution*, and joined the communist party. After a number of affairs, Reich left Fink for Elsa Lindenburg, a choreographer and dance therapist. Elsa, like Laura Perls, studied with Elsa Gindler, who was promoting attention to the body as an aid to healing.

For Reich, psychology and politics were not divisible. The source of neurosis might be found in the economic or social conditions of the patient. Reflecting later on his experience at this time in both his private and public practice, he observed that:

> Neither the psychiatrist nor the psychoanalyst thought to inquire into the social living conditions of the patients. It was known, of course, that there was poverty and material distress, but somehow this was not regarded as being relevant to the treatment. Yet the patient's material conditions were a constant problem in the clinic. It was often necessary to provide social first aid ... There was a tremendous gap between private practice and practice in the clinic. (Reich 1993: 75)

As he became more politically active, his frustration with the psychoanalytic community for their failure to take account of social deprivation as a factor in mental illness was matched by his frustration at the blindness to the psychological dimension exhibited by fellow communists, who 'never tired of telling me that the sexual etiology of psychic illness was a bourgeois whim, that it was "only material distress" which produced neuroses' (Reich 1993: 78). Reich observed a vicious circle of physical and psychological suffering.

> [I]t is the neuroses of these people that ruins their ability to do something sensible about their distress, to assert themselves more effectively, to stand up to the competition of the labour market, to come to an understanding with others who are in a similar social situation, to keep their heads clear for rational thinking. (Reich 1993: 78)

This may sound like common sense, but Reich was battling with two rival and equally rigid orthodoxies: 'Reich was not only a Freudian renegade; he was Marxist revisionist. He tried combining Freudian ideas with Marxist ones, an enterprise that soon got him expelled from both the International Psychoanalytic Association and the German Communist Party' (Anderson 2004: 92).

Nazis and muscular armour

Reich's political concerns and his interest in psychic healing came together in his focus on the body, which came to dominate his therapeutic approach. He had come to believe that people develop what he called muscular armour or characterological armour, which serves the purpose of keeping potentially explosive emotions in, distancing them from the emotions of others, and protecting them not only from intolerable feelings of anger, rage and grief, but also from joy and fuller sexual expression. This concept of muscular armour was, in part at least, a response to the frightening advance of fascism. Psychological health, Reich believed, involves a full-body emotional response to life. And for Reich, the social and political dimensions were inescapable:

> The character structure of modern man, who reproduces a six-thousand-year-old patriarchal authoritarian culture, is typified by characterological armouring against his inner nature and against the social misery which surrounds him. The characterological armouring is the basis of isolation, indigence, craving for authority, fear of responsibility, mystic longing, sexual misery, and neurotically impotent rebelliousness, as was all pathological intolerance. Man has alienated himself from, and has grown hostile toward, life. (Reich 1993: 7)

Reich's orgone accumulator is no longer taken seriously; his focus on the orgasm in psychic healing and his belief that healing is dependent on genital gratification remains controversial, certainly in the way Reich included it in therapy. But his experiments with other kinds of physical release, kicking and punching, deep breathing, screaming and assuming different postures to evoke a range of emotions, have filtered into the mainstream.

Although Reich had died in a federal penitentiary in 1957, his influence was strongly felt at the Esalen Institute in the 1960s (Chapter 2). Two of the most prominent figures at Esalen, Fritz Perls and Will Schutz, had both drawn inspiration from him. Perhaps his greatest legacy, however, comes from his theoretical writings about the relationship of psychology to society, contributing to a widespread shift in attitudes towards sexuality. He is also credited with being the first somatic coach.

The somatic legacy

While Reich was subverting his psychoanalytic training to focus on the body, others, approaching from the other direction, were exploring the psychic dimension of physical health. During the 1920s Ida Rolf was creating a system, now known as Rolfing, of releasing emotions stored in the body through deep massage and manipulation of the connective tissue overlying the muscles. One of Rolf's students was Joseph Heller, who originated Hellerwork, which combines the physical with the emotional, adding dialogue with the patient to the practice of breaking down muscle patterns, to release trapped emotions.

Reich's own work directly inspired a tradition of somatic therapy.

Alexander Lowen

Reich's most prominent student was Alexander Lowen (1910–2008), who had graduated from Brooklyn Law School before retraining as a therapist. He studied with Reich in New York in the 1940s and early 1950s. Later he and a colleague John Pierrakos developed a form of mind–body therapy called Bioenergetic Analysis. He established his practice in Connecticut, where he founded the International Institute for Bioenergetic Analysis. Lowen credited Reich with clearing the path for this kind of work, arguing that the very problems that Freudian analysis proposed to deal with, such as hysterical paralysis, could not be adequately treated with an exclusively verbal approach:

> Although psychoanalysis is regarded as a discipline limited to the study of psychic problems, it had its origin in the problems of disturbed somatic functioning, the etiology of which could not be ascribed to organic damage ... The solution was not possible until Reich formulated the basic law of emotional life: that is, the unity and synthesis of psychosomatic functioning. (Lowen 1958: 19)

Lowen believed in a balanced and interconnected combination of physical exercises and analysis. In Bioenergetics, patients are taught to experience emotions by adopting different postures and breathing patterns. The experience is then discussed with the patient. The essential analytical assumptions in Bioenergetics are Freudian in nature: feelings expressed during body work are believed to be repressed emotions originating in childhood. But Lowen's interest in the body grew out of an awareness of the limitation of conventional analysis:

> The problem which psychoanalysis faces arises from the fact that the analyst deals with body sensations and body feelings on a verbal and

mental level, for the subject matter of analysis is the feeling and behavior of the individual. His ideas, fantasies and dreams are explored only as a means to comprehend and reach the feelings and to influence the behavior. Can we not conceive the possibility that there are other ways and means to changes feelings and actions? (Lowen 1958: x)

Richard Strozzi-Heckler

Another practitioner influenced by Reich was Richard Strozzi-Heckler (1944–). Raised in a military family in the late 1940s and 1950s, Strozzi-Heckler was an accomplished student athlete and a martial arts expert with a black belt in aikido. He served in the marines in the mid-60s, then travelled in Asia where he studied yoga and meditation. In 1970, with a PhD in clinical psychology, he drew on his experience of physical activities to co-found a school of body-oriented psychotherapy called Lomi Work. In the 1980s he was involved in a project with the US Army to test how a variety of practices, including meditation, might contribute to training. He developed this work into a methodology called Strozzi Somatics that could be applied to groups of civilians. He is associated with the concept of embodied leadership, which identifies certain physical behaviours, including posture, expression and tone of voice. The assumption is that these behaviours can be practised and that improvements to leadership performance will follow.

Fernando Flores and Julio Olalla

One of Strozzi-Heckler's collaborators in the 1980s and 1990s was Fernando Flores (1943–), who added his research to Strozzi-Heckler's somatic approach. Flores also worked during this period with Werner Erhard, the founder of *est*, contributing ideas on language and its effects to Erhard's training curriculum (Chapter 3). Flores had served as finance minister in Allende's government in Chile and, after the coup, had been held as a political prisoner for three years by the Pinochet regime. Later, in the USA, he connected with another Chilean who had also been forced into exile, Julio Olalla (1945–). Olalla had been a student in Chile of Humberto Maturana (1928–), a groundbreaking biologist and philosopher who, with neuroscientist Francisco Varela (1946–2001), had made a powerful scientific case for the role of biology in shaping our understanding of ourselves and of reality. According to Maturana and Varela, we are structurally determined as human beings. Our 'knowing' is rooted in our biology, and 'reality' for the individual is not outside, but rather inside the body.

Together Flores and Olalla were key figures in the development of what we know of today as ontological coaching. Ontology is the study of being and ontological coaching is focused on the relationship of feelings and the essence of what it means to be human to the body. Ontological coaches speak of the soul as the essence of identity, locating soul usually at the intersection of language, emotions and physiology. 'This is the core of our existence, defining who we are, what is deeply meaningful, and what is and is not possible for us' (Seiler 2003: 10). In this way they challenge the traditional mind–body split of Western philosophy and the theological division of body and soul, reconfiguring the body as an essential contributing element of human identity in its most profound sense.

Implications for coaching

1. Encourage your client to become aware of what she is feeling, experiencing and noticing about herself and her environment.
2. As a coach, it is important also to be conscious of your own somatic reactions as you work with your client.
3. While attending to your client's physical bearing and responses, don't overlook her language and her emotional tone.
4. Body work and ontological coaching encourage us, as practitioners, to expand our own range of movements and emotions when coaching.
5. This approach to coaching involves listening with a particular kind of attention to your client, tuning in to her tone of voice, pace, breathing and rhythm.

Chapter 8: Searching for wholeness: Fritz Perls and gestalt

The gestalt approach is holistic, phenomenological, existential and humanistic. Gestalt theory and practice have been a wonderful resource for me as a coach. I challenge my client to look in the mirror; to become aware of her behaviour and how it influences others. We brainstorm together about alternative ways of thinking and behaving in a difficult situation – and then, together, we observe the outcome.

As a coach and gestaltist I listen deeply to, and enter into, an intense dialogue with my client. What is the concern or the hope of my client? What is in the foreground? – in the background? I become aware of the process – of what is said and what is not said. I observe the use of her voice, breath, gestures and postures. This deep and phenomenological listening is helpful in creating rapport with the client, building the relationship, and co-creating a field between us where change is possible. Pushing change will only increase the resistance in the client. We must create space and allow change to happen. The gestalt paradoxical theory of change says that when I push too hard for change, it won't happen. Change happens when we stop pushing and dance in the moment together.

I use questions to evoke new awareness; to encourage experimenting with new behaviour and gain new experience. As a coach I observe, reflect and report my awareness, and observe what happens – for both of us. Experience is closer to truth than thought, and emotion is stronger than rationality when they pull in different directions.

The goal of gestalt is becoming aware of how we inhibit being who we are and achieving the results we want. How do we do that? When we know how, we have a chance to try out other ways, learn, experience and act differently.

Marianne Borg Hyökki, ScD, MA, PCC
Helsinki, Finland
Quantum Business Coaching
http://www.coachmarianne.com
http://www.businesscoaching.fi

Fritz Perls does his thing

Born in Germany, Fritz Perls (1893–1970) fought in the First World War, was involved in radical politics and the experimental art movements in 1920s Berlin, and migrated to South Africa to escape the Nazi regime, before moving to New York and from there to California. Along the way he rejected his Freudian psychoanalytic training. He drew inspiration from Wilhelm Reich's body work and some of the insights of gestalt psychology and, with his wife Laura, constructed a new approach to therapy.

Gestalt psychologists do not regard gestalt therapy as a branch of their discipline. As Mary Henle put it, in her 1975 presidential address to members of the American Psychological Association:

> What Perls has done has been to take a few terms from gestalt psychology, stretch their meaning beyond recognition, mix them with notions – often unclear and often incompatible – from the depth psychologies, existentialism, and common sense, and he has called the whole mixture gestalt therapy. His work has no substantive relation to scientific gestalt psychology. To use his own language, Fritz Perls has done 'his thing'; whatever it is, it is not gestalt psychology. (Henle 1986: 22–35)

As a maverick intellectual, at war with the dominance of the intellect over the senses, and who pushed the boundaries of therapeutic theory and practice, Perls finally found his spiritual home at Esalen in the mid-1960s (Chapter 2). Though old enough to be a grandfather to the generation most involved in the counter-culture, he was an influential figure. His slogan 'Lose your mind and come to your senses' precisely fitted the ethos of that time and place. He summed up his belief that people should do what they feel rather than what they ought in his *Gestalt Prayer*, which essentially says that everyone should do their own thing and, if as a result, people connect, that is great. 'If not, it can't be helped' (http://www.fritzperls.com/gestaltprayer/). This prayer can be found easily on the internet, though, significantly, popular quotation sites tend to omit the last line, which suggests a desire to soften the more acerbic aspect of Perls' attitude.

Early struggles

In 1969 Perls wrote a chronology of his life (http://www.gestalt.org/fritz. htm). It looks like jottings but has distinctly formal elements. The writing is emotionally engaged but with a sense of irony at the expense of his younger self. Summarized in these few pages is a remarkable life story touched by some of the major political, social and intellectual events of the twentieth century.

Perls' interest in psychology, and his rebellion against imposed values, show up early on. At 17, he's unable to conquer 'forbidden sex'. A psychiatrist prescribes 'bromides and exercise', advice he rejects. At 18 he's discovering poetry, philosophy and theatre: 'Canvas and painted props are out. Three dimensions. Make the stage real. Turn the world into a stage. What is reality? Confusing.' Confusion echoes through the narrative like a refrain. He rejects law as a career, in spite of having a famous uncle in the profession, and considers psychology 'nonsense'. Knowledge of Freud who 'sees sex problem' draws him towards medicine. He survives the 'agony' of trench warfare, but describes himself as 'desensitised'. After the war he's 'rebelliously involved in politics' which leaves him 'very confused' then joins bohemian artists, '. . . creating a new world. Bauhaus, [the expressionist painter] Brücke, Dadaism'.

It's principally a record of his intellectual development. Major life events take a subordinate place. For example, his escape from Germany to the Netherlands in 1933 and then, in the following year, to South Africa, gets only this phlegmatic sentence – 'An early refugee from the Hitler regime.'

The earliest reference to Reich, who would influence the physical dimension in gestalt therapy, is in 1925: 'Started seven years of useless couch life. Felt I was stupid. Finally Wilhelm Reich, then still sane, made some sense.' The seeds of a breakthrough into a gestalt approach were sown in the following year, when Perls was working in Frankfurt, but he was not yet fully receptive: 'Kurt Goldstein, Frankfurt neurologist. Genius neuro-psychiatrist. Organism-as-a-whole concept. Makes much sense, but I, still involved and loyal to the Freudians, resist him. Confusing.'

Perls' mentor, Kurt Goldstein (1878–1965), a professor of neurology, had specialized in the study of traumatic brain injuries during the First World War, when there was a sudden glut of suitable patients. In their work together he introduced Perls to ideas related to gestalt psychology. Gestalt in German means something like 'the form' or 'wholeness' of something. A basic gestalt concept is that the mind is programmed to perceive things in their wholeness. We naturally seek to make sense of what we're looking at, even if that involves constructing a coherent image on the basis of incomplete evidence, or, in exceptional circumstances, selecting between two equally possible images. Classic illustrations of this tendency are the chalice that might be two faces in profile, and the young woman who could be an old crone. From a single line on a flat plane we deduce a three dimensional form. From an ambiguous set of marks, we select one meaning. This is what the mind does. It completes the picture. It rejects ambiguity by choosing one thing to focus on at the expense of another. It distinguishes between an object and its background. In gestalt terms, it finds a *figure* to stand out against the *ground*.

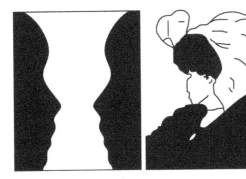

Solving the mind–body problem

For Perls, this way of thinking was appealing, but didn't yet provide the answer he was looking for. He had become interested in the role of the body in mental health: 'Wife Laura involved in expressive movement – Gindler. No integration yet of soma and psyche. Mind-body relationship still confusing.' Elsa Gindler was a pioneer of somatic bodywork, which emphasized self-observation and physical awareness. Her influence would later show up in Perls' own practice. But at this point Perls was still engaged in orthodox analysis – his 'useless couch life' – and apparently struggling as much to achieve his own sense of wholeness as to put these ideas together intellectually.

Six years later, having settled in South Africa, he was in Germany for the Freudian congress in Marienbad. The rejection of a paper of his as unorthodox made him 'resentful'. He was thrown into a 'turmoil of confusion', but emerged with a new sense of certainty, a newfound confidence that he could challenge the doctrines of Freud and his loyal disciples. 'I know better. What? Me know better than the Gods? Yes, yes, yes.'

Back in South Africa, still enmeshed in a therapeutic method that seemed increasingly unsatisfactory, and struggling 'to get out of the quicksand of free associations,' he returned uncertainly to ideas he'd learned from Goldstein. The breakthrough, when it comes, is credited to Jan Smuts, the Prime Minister of South Africa, a philosopher by training who, in addition to founding the League of Nations, had coined the term *holistic*. 'Jan Smuts has the answer: ecology. Organism-as-a-whole-embedded-in-environment.'

He determined that the Freudians, in reducing the mind to its component parts and seeking to solve problems that are rooted in a lack of integration by an exclusively mental process, had got things upside down. Analysis, by encouraging clients to look at themselves in a reflective way, rather than being spontaneously aware of their current reality, actually increased neurosis: 'Freud's catharsis notion is the emerging gestalt. Not in the Unconscious, but right on the surface. The obvious is put on the throne. The neurotic is a person who is blind to the obvious.'

Gestalt according to Perls

Like other organisms, as long as we're healthily aware of our environment, we draw from it what we need for our continuing health. But it's harder for humans. Perls' analysis of the particular human issue has been expressed like this:

> [O]ur complexity can muddy the waters of the simple need-satisfaction equation. We can suppress some needs and overemphasize others; or our idea of survival can get warped, so we believe we must maintain ourselves in a certain way, even if to an outsider what we are doing is stupid. Our dominant need becomes connected totally with our sense of self, but it is a sense of self that is no longer fluid or elastic, a neurotic self. It has stopped being aware. (Butler-Bowdon 2007: 218)

Perls' first book, *Ego, Hunger and Aggression*, was published in 1942. According to him, it emerged from a kind of automatic writing: 'I am teaching myself touch typing, slowly, getting bored. Why not let thoughts flow onto sheets of paper? Doing so, I discover idea after idea.'

During the Second World War, Perls served in the South African army as a psychiatrist, where his line of work was not much respected: 'At first, the internists say: Behind every neurosis is a stomach ulcer. But in the end they say: Perls, you are right. Behind the ulcer is the neurosis.'

The term *gestalt therapy* was coined in 1950 and publicly launched in a book co-written with Paul Goodman and journalist Ralph Hefferline. Perls became increasingly interested in working with groups rather than individuals, considering it more effective. He moved to Esalen in 1964 (Chapter 2), finding that 'What the Bauhaus was in Germany for the creation of a new style in architecture and the arts, Esalen is as a practical centre of the third wave of humanistic psychology' (http://www.gestalt.org/fritz.htm).

Perls favoured what he called *contact* – any direct encounter with our environment or expressive engagement with it. *Confluence*, in contrast, was his term for acting out of habit or on instruction. He thought of *responsibility* as deadening and neurotic, preferring *earnestness,* the quality of absolute focus and attention that children bring to their play, a state that is compatible with curiosity, spontaneity and imagination. In Perls' view, the 'gestalt outlook is the original, undistorted, natural approach to life; that is, to man's thinking, acting, feeling. The average person, having been raised in an atmosphere full of splits, has lost his Wholeness, his Integrity' (Butler-Bowdon 2007: 218).

Perls' techniques were aggressive, his manner could be sarcastic, and therapy with him was often raw and humiliating. He felt that therapy was hard work and he made fun of people looking for joy or ecstasy. According to one account:

> The object of gestalt work, Fritz sometimes said, was not to achieve a breakthrough; rather, it was to achieve a break-in, a sudden invasion of one's own privacy, a re-established contact with lost and deadened feelings. Fritz was confident that this could be achieved in a single session if the patient was ready to let it happen . . . Intellectualizing – thinking and analyzing – came in for much abuse in Fritz's sessions . . . He could, and often did, permit his patients to make fools of themselves. (Anderson 2004: 97–8)

Writing in 1976, Perls gave an example of his somewhat idiosyncratic, therapeutic style:

> Okay. I would like you to put phoniness in that chair: talk to phoniness . . . Now let's finish up by putting that smirk in the chair. Talk to your smirk . . . Put the old man [in the dream] in that chair and compare him to me. What are the similarities, what are the differences? . . . Can you talk to that memory once more? Change seats. Be the memory . . . Say, bye-bye memory. (Perls in Rowan 1993: 100–10)

Current gestalt techniques

As currently practised, gestalt therapy emphasizes what the client is experiencing, thinking and doing in the present moment. It focuses on the social and environmental context and the kind of adjustments the client is making to it. The purpose is to free the client from unfinished business that is preventing her from being more spontaneously and creatively alive. Talk is often replaced by experiment, physical activity and dramatic expression. A client dealing with feelings about a judgemental parent, for example, might bring the parent imaginatively into the room and address him directly. The therapist isn't seen as fixing the client but sharing in the creation of a process that is rooted in the here-and-now. It is easy to see why a gestalt approach is considered relevant to coaching.

Implications for coaching

1. In the same way that gestalt therapy focuses on the process – the totality of what is happening in the room – as coaches we need to pay attention to the client's behaviour, body movements and energy, and to unexpressed feelings.
2. Gestalt bears a resemblance to 'mindfulness' practice. In any coaching engagement it is important to be attuned to the client's feelings and perceptions.
3. Gestalt theory encourages a phenomenological approach. As a coach, your role is to observe and feed back to the client what is happening in the space between you, and in the 'field' in which you are both working.
4. Observe the client's breathing, posture and other non-verbal behaviour. If you feel comfortable doing so, ask him to exaggerate the behaviour to help him understand himself more fully.
5. Ask the client to imagine that someone she is having issues with is sitting in the room. Have her speak directly to the empty chair. Invite her to occupy the chair, and speak from that person's point of view.
6. Remember the concept of paradoxical change: the more the client attempts to be who he is not, the more he will remain the same.

Chapter 9: From neurosis to ecstasy: humanistic and transpersonal psychology

Humanistic psychology sets the stage for how we enter the coach–client relationship. My client and I create a two-way relationship based on openness, honesty and trust. We enter an agreement that establishes us as equals in a partnership for the client's success and we view the client as whole and complete. Most importantly, I hold the client in unconditional positive regard. Believing in a client and his worth and capability, even when he may not see this in himself, sets the foundation for the coaching relationship. For me, unconditional positive regard is the key to establishing the coaching agreement and a relationship of trust with the client. In doing so we create a safe environment that encourages trust, accepts the client for who he is, reminds us to withhold judgement, and supports the development of deep dialogue.

It's not easy to be without judgement, and remaining neutral is crucial. I work physically or virtually in the organization working with individuals, leaders or teams. I hear the stories and folklore that permeate the organization. Stories can influence any coach's ability to work effectively with the client. Unconditional positive regard allows for a higher level of focus and keeps me out of the stories. It's a principle I can share with the client to see beyond surface behaviours and situations as he works with others. Authentically appreciating the humanness of others is a powerful and necessary exercise.

Diane Brennan, MBA, MCC
Tucson, Arizona, USA
Brennan Associates Coaching and Consulting
diane@coachdiane.com
http://www.coachdiane.com

When I began coaching executives in 1990 and the two decades that have followed, I began applying tools and techniques from my PhD in *transpersonal psychology* and practices to raise my client's consciousness, open his mind, and reveal untapped potential through a combination of ancient practices (meditation, Tai Chi) and modern applications (guided imagery, mindfulness, metaphor and journaling). I use various tools in my life and in my coaching practice on a regular basis. I offer and teach techniques such as mindfulness (aka meditation) to my clients to increase focus, to become present in the moment, and to learn to *respond* to life's challenges rather than *reacting*, as is more common.

I also use guided imagery to have clients access their untapped unconscious creativity to current challenges/goals, and have them access what Assagioli called sub-personalities . . . parts of their inner self that can aid or hinder their process of personal and business development. Additionally, I often use a technique from Fritz Perls (gestalt therapy) that he called *the empty chair* . . . (some today equate Voice Dialogue to this approach). The client can put different voices in his life in separate chairs and have a dialogue with them back and forth. This can also be done by phone coaching by simply asking the client to do the same in her office. In essence, it is fairly easy to introduce techniques that have evolved from transpersonal psychology and the ancient traditions that were tapped in coaching today.

Patrick Williams, EdD, MCC, BCC
Palm Coast, Florida, USA
Certified Wellness Professional (National Wellness Institute)
Founder, Institute for Life Coach Training and Coaching the Global Village
http://www.lifecoachtraining.com
http://www.CoachingTheGlobalVillage.org

Arrange whatever pieces come your way.

Virginia Woolf

Carl Rogers and the birth of humanistic psychology

During the 1930s and 1940s, when Carl Rogers was teaching and researching at Rochester, Ohio State and Chicago, the field of psychology was dominated by Freudians and behaviourists. Rogers' findings and theories, which were first published in *Client-Centered Therapy* (1951), announced a radical departure from received wisdom. Of all psychologists, Rogers, who is credited with being one of the primary founders of the humanistic (person-centred) approach, is the one who most influenced the discipline of coaching.

At a time when the vast majority of the literature and practice was based on Freudian or neo-Freudian principles, therapy involved delving into a patient's past, uncovering painful childhood experiences, and relying on the professional to guide the patient towards understanding and recovery; or it sidestepped the role of the mind altogether to focus directly on modifying observable behaviour. Rogers challenged these approaches. Patients were to be treated with a new level of dignity and considered equal participants in the process. It was to be assumed that they had the ability to understand their own problems and a capacity for healing and growth.

Carl Rogers (1908–1970) was born in Chicago, the fourth of six children. As an undergraduate he studied agriculture, then history. He intended to join the ministry, but after two years of training he went instead to Columbia teachers college where he studied for his doctorate.

Two major influences on his thinking were Martin Buber and Otto Rank. Martin Buber (1878–1965) was an existential philosopher who developed a philosophy of dialogue. In his best known essay *I and Thou*, published in 1925, Buber discusses the crucial nature of the space between two people in a conscious discussion where each person is regarding the other as an equal. Otto Rank (1884–1939) is famous among therapists, artists and religious teachers for being one of the first Freudian-trained psychoanalysts to break with Freud's teachings. Best known for his books *The Trauma of Birth* (1929) and *Art and Artist* (1932), Rank stressed the importance of the client and therapist working together in the 'here and now'; the necessary tension between separation and connectedness for all human beings; and the importance of understanding human development as a lifelong construction.

In 1936, while Rogers was teaching in Rochester, he invited Otto Rank to give a series of lectures on Rank's post-Freudian models of experiential and relational therapy. Rogers was deeply affected by these lectures and Rank's thinking. He credited Rank with having profoundly influenced his concept of client-centred therapy and the entire profession of counselling (http://www.ottorank.com/).

Rogers was not the only therapist influenced by Rank's ideas. Fritz Perls and the gestalt therapists based their approach to gestalt on the 'here-and-now' approach of Otto Rank. Later gestalt writers credited Rank with first advocating a personal interaction between therapist and client, and the importance of observing and describing what was happening between the two of them at the moment.

Between Rank's lecture and the publication of *Client-Centered Therapy* came 15 years of clinical practice and research during which Rogers' ideas were shaped. These years also saw the fulfilment of the Nazi ideology in Europe and all the horrors of the Second World War. No doubt these events undermined some people's faith in human nature. For others it gave the search for meaning an added urgency.

The client-centred approach

Published in 1951, Carl Rogers' *Client-Centered Therapy* established the core principles of humanistic treatment. These are well known, but are worth reiterating:

1. The client, not the therapist, is at the centre of the therapeutic experience.
2. Trust between client and therapist, and empathy for the client, are essential to the success of the therapeutic engagement. This requires the therapist to accurately sense the client's experience and to communicate both understanding and acceptance.
3. The therapist's job is not to fix clients but to listen absolutely to what they are saying.
4. The therapist–client relationship is truthful when it includes the moods and feelings of the practitioner. The presence of the therapist in the fullest sense is crucial to the process.
5. The goal in humanistic therapy is for the client to be able to own all aspects of him or herself.
6. When a client experiences his or her authentic self, contradictory feelings may arise. This is part of the process. The real danger is in denying parts of ourselves.
7. Being open to concepts and values that vary from one's own is vital to learning. The therapist should encourage clients to be open-minded.

Rogers described his own practice in these terms:

> When I am at my best, as a group facilitator or a therapist, I discover another characteristic. I find that when I am closest to my inner, intuitive self, when I am somehow in touch with the unknown in me, when perhaps I am in a slightly altered state of consciousness in the relationship, then whatever I do seems to be full of healing. Then simply my presence is releasing and when I can relax and be close to the transcendental core of me, then I may behave in strange and impulsive ways in the relationship, ways which I cannot justify rationally, which have nothing to do with my thought processes. But these strange behaviors turn out to be right, in some odd way . . . Our relationship transcends itself and becomes a part of something larger. Profound growth and healing and energy are present. (Rogers, quoted in Kirschenbaum and Henderson 1989: 137)

The central hypothesis of humanistic psychology is that the individual has within herself resources for self-understanding, for altering her self-concept, changing her attitudes and self-directing her behaviour. These resources can be tapped through skilful facilitation and a climate that promotes respect for the individual. Coaching depends on an equal partnership between client and coach. Given the qualities of humanistic psychology, it is easy to see why its precepts are central to current coaching practice.

Victor Frankl and the creation of meaning

Austrian psychiatrist Viktor Frankl (1905–1997) had worked during the 1930s in the General Hospital in Vienna, directing the so-called 'suicide pavilion' in which were housed women prone to suicide. In his professional capacity he was no stranger to human suffering. In the early years of the war he practised neurosurgery in the Rothschild Hospital, the only Viennese hospital still admitting Jews. In 1942 he and his wife were sent to the Theresienstadt concentration camp in Czechoslovakia. He was later moved to Auschwitz and from there to Dachau. His wife died in Bergen-Belsen. Frankl survived to be freed by allied soldiers. A year later he published (in German) the book that was later to become widely known under the title *Man's Search for Meaning*.

Reflecting on his intimate encounters with despair, Frankl concluded that a sense of purpose – a belief that you have something to accomplish in life – is essential for survival, whether in a concentration camp or not. 'There is nothing in the world, I venture to say, that would so effectively help one to survive even the worst conditions as the knowledge that there is meaning in one's life. There is much wisdom in the words of Nietzsche: '"He who has a *why* to live for can bear almost any *how*." I can see in these words a motto which holds true for any psychotherapy' (Frankl 2004: 109). He argues that if you can't change your circumstances, you can change your perception of them, and writes of the uniquely human potential . . . to turn an individual's predicament into a human achievement.

Early in his career Frankl had been influenced by Freud and Adler. *Man's Search for Meaning* is a radical departure from Freudian assumptions:

> I consider it a dangerous misconception of mental hygiene to assume that what man needs in the first place is equilibrium or, as it is called in biology, 'homeostasis' . . . What man actually needs is not a tensionless state but rather the striving and struggling for a worthwhile goal, a freely chosen task. What he needs is not the discharge of tension at any cost but the call of a potential meaning waiting to be fulfilled by him. (Frankl 2004: 110)

As a record of life in the camps, *Man's Search for Meaning* was, and remains, a powerful and important document. In its time it also played a significant role in popularizing a humanistic and aspirational approach to therapeutic practice and the understanding of human motivation. The book is timeless, and I believe that it teaches us two important coaching principles: 1) emphasize choice; and 2) identify your life purpose.

Abraham Maslow and the search for transcendence

Rogers seems to have had a fairly cheerful and emotionally benign upbringing. Abraham Maslow (1908–1970), in contrast, grew up the oldest of seven children in a family atmosphere that was filled with tension and anger. In particular, he had a deeply conflicted relationship with his mother, whom he characterized as stingy, selfish, prejudiced and self-centred. As a child of Russian Jewish immigrants, he experienced anti-Semitism from his teachers and from the other children in the neighbourhood. In spite of this – or because of it – he developed a theory of psychology and psychological practices based on the assumption of goodness in all human beings and the ability of anyone to develop a healthy attitude in life:

> Every age but ours has had its model, its hero. All these have been given us by our culture; the hero, the gentleman, the knight, the mystic. About all we have left is the well-adjusted man without problems, a very pale and doubtful substitute. Perhaps we shall soon be able to use as our guide and model the fully growing and self-fulfilling human being, the one in whom all his potentialities are coming to full development, the one whose inner nature expresses itself freely, rather than being warped, repressed or denied. (Maslow 1968, 3rd ed.: 5)

Maslow, who studied psychology at the City College of New York and the University of Wisconsin, placed himself broadly in the Freudian tradition but was interested in more positive outcomes. Whereas Freudian analysis was designed to deal only with the sick part of the psychological spectrum, Maslow aspired to enhance the healthy part. In this he was closer to Alfred Adler than to Freud.

Alfred Adler (1870–1937) was one of the originators of depth psychology – a practice which explores the relationship between the conscious and the unconscious. He split with Freud, arguing for a more holistic view of the individual. Adler emphasized the importance of equality in family relationships. He favoured a democratic approach to raising children. He considered self-esteem to be important and developed the concept of the inferiority complex. Maslow, too, advocated the importance of self-esteem:

> [Maslow] subscribed to some Freudian ideas, but not all. Instead of adopting Freud's pessimistic stance, [he] chose to see the grander side

of human nature. Instead of placing human beings in a struggle between id, ego, and superego, he focused on human potential, integrity, and peak experiences ... Finally, rather than denigrating religion as illusionary, he regarded transcendental experiences as legitimate and potentially healthy expressions. Like Freud, he was a child of science, but unlike Freud, he made room for the mystical. (Wood 2010: 140)

Another influence on Maslow's thinking was the anthropologist Ruth Benedict (1887–1948). In her groundbreaking work, *Patterns of Culture* (1934), Benedict had made the case for cultural relativism, arguing that cultures have their own customs and moral systems that should be respected rather than judged, and proposed that different cultures could be thought of as having personalities, analogous to human personalities, whose qualities individuals are expected to reflect.

Maslow's hierarchy of needs

In his book *Motivation and Personality* (1954), Maslow proposed a model of human needs, in which five stages of need – both physical and psychological – are placed in a hierarchy, according to how essential they are. This is commonly pictured as a pyramid, though Maslow did not present it this way. And although the more basic needs are placed towards the bottom and the more rarefied ones further up, Maslow stressed that progress up the pyramid is not necessarily linear. Growth may occur simultaneously at different levels. It's a mistake to assume that the needs on one level must be met before a person can begin achieving fulfilment on another, higher one:

Maslow's hierarchy of needs

Self-actualization
Personal growth and fulfilment
Need for self-esteem and esteem from others
Achievement, status, responsibility, reputation
Love and belongingness
Family, affection, relationships, work group
Need for safety and security
Protection, security, order, law, limits, stability
Biological and physiological needs
Air, food, water, shelter, warmth, sex, sleep

> If we define growth as the various processes which bring the person toward ultimate self-actualization, then this conforms better with the observed fact that it is going on all the time in the life history. It discourages also the stepwise, all or none, salutatory conception of motivational progression toward self-actualization in which the basic needs are completely gratified, one by one, before the next higher one emerges into consciousness. (Maslow 1968, 2nd ed.: 26)

Self-actualization was Maslow's term for the highest state of human development, and he believed that the potential to achieve it was inherent in all human beings. Self-actualized individuals, according to Maslow, devote themselves to a vocation, to what he called 'being' values – truth, beauty, goodness and simplicity. He developed this theory in *Toward a Psychology of Being* (1968). To make self-actualization a less esoteric concept, Maslow laid out a definition of how a self-actualized person would function on a daily basis. These qualities included the following: an enhanced ability to perceive reality; an increased acceptance of self, of others and of nature; a greater ability to act spontaneously; a tendency to be more problem-centred as opposed to ego-centred (meaning that one focuses on achieving tasks and life-missions for their own sake); increased detachment and desire for privacy; increased autonomy, and resistance to enculturation; a greater freshness of appreciation, and richness of emotional reaction; an increased identification with the human species; improved interpersonal relations; a more democratic character structure; and greatly increased creativity (Maslow 1968, 2nd ed.: 26).

Peak experiences

One of the marks of the self-actualized individual is a higher frequency of peak experiences. A peak experience is essentially a sudden feeling of intense happiness and well-being; a feeling of wholeness, of integration of the self and the world. Such experiences are, Maslow believed, rare, mystical, exciting, deeply moving and exhilarating. According to Maslow, the term peak experience refers to:

> the mystic, or oceanic, or nature experience, the aesthetic perception, the creative moment, the therapeutic or intellectual insight, the orgasmic experience, certain forms of athletic fulfilment, etc. These and other moments of highest happiness and fulfilment I shall call the peak-experiences. (Maslow 1968, 2nd ed.: 73)

Qualities associated with peak-experiences include: wholeness, perfection, completion, justice, aliveness, richness, simplicity, beauty, goodness, uniqueness, effortlessness, playfulness, truth and self-sufficiency. According to

Maslow, peak experiences cannot be created, only experienced at moments in one's life. His studies of peak experiences reinforced his conclusions that self-actualization experiences occurred in many situations:

> Ecstatic and mystical experiences – those joyous, serene, wondrous moments – occurred, Maslow explained, during ordinary and extraordinary moments, from the profound contentment one woman felt sitting with her child and husband at the breakfast table to intellectual achievements, sexual encounters, musical performances, and mountain hikes. Interpreting these stories as a nineteenth-century romantic might describe a 'sublime' moment, he concluded that peak experiences provoked great exhilaration and loss of time and space. They transformed and strengthened while bringing a kind of satisfaction that 'the universe is all of a piece and that one has a place in it – one is part of it, and one belongs to it. (Wood 2010: 159)

Due to his interest in mystical experiences, the British novelist Aldous Huxley was an influence. In the acknowledgements to his book, *Toward A Psychology of Being*, Maslow notes that Huxley was among the first to convince him that he should examine the psychology of religion and mysticism.

There is also a clear connection between Maslow's interest in the peak experience and the transcendental explorations of later contemporaries such as Alan Watts, Alan Ginsberg and Ram Dass. Through different routes, spiritual seekers, humanist psychologists and body workers were all striving towards similar goals. In his thinking, Maslow was anticipating the concept of a transpersonal psychology.

A meeting of minds

In the late 1950s Maslow had convened meetings with Carl Rogers, Rollo May and other psychologists that led to the establishment of the *Journal of Humanistic Psychology*. In 1963 the American Association for Humanistic Psychology held its first national convention in Philadelphia. Five assumptions were established as central to humanistic psychology: the whole person is more than the sum of his or her parts; we are affected by our relationships with others; a person is naturally aware; a person has choice and responsibility; a person is intentional and inclined to look for meaning.

Rogers and Maslow were allies in this enterprise. But it's worth reflecting briefly on the differences between them. Although both are deeply interested in the development of human potential, Rogers puts more emphasis on the nature and presence of the therapist in promoting transformation. In *On Becoming a Person*, which was to become his most famous book, Rogers wrote: 'the paradoxical aspect of my experience is that the more I am simply willing to be myself, in all this complexity of life, and the more I am willing to understand and accept the realities in myself and in the other person, the more change seems to be stirred up' (Rogers 1961: 22).

Sometimes, in his writings, I think that Rogers puts too much faith in the ability of the therapist to effect change simply by 'being' – relaxing into himself or herself and allowing the connection with the client to occur. This method worked brilliantly for Rogers. But Rogers was an exceptional individual, with a remarkable skill in creating connection and healing. Not all psychologists or coaches have this exquisite touch. In practice, it may be that telling a coach or psychologist to connect to his or her inner self, on the assumption that trust and healing will naturally follow, glosses over what it takes to work skilfully with people, and how much intention must go into building an effective therapeutic or coaching relationship.

Maslow, a theorist and researcher, was less of a practitioner than Rogers, and he has less to say about how clinicians should work with clients. He places a tremendous emphasis on the capacity of individuals to heal themselves, but the process by which this happens is less clearly explained. Between them, however, these two men transformed the field of psychology. They shared a profound belief in the capacity for human growth, and the generosity and optimism of their vision found an eagerly receptive audience. Their work laid the most basic foundation for what we do in coaching today.

The origins of transpersonal psychology

Maslow's interest in higher levels of awareness, and particularly his research into peak experiences, was of particular interest to a new breed of psychologists interested in what they called the 'transpersonal' dimension. These transpersonal psychologists were taking a particular interest in creativity, intuitive insights and mystical glimpses of the eternal or the connectedness of things. They were integrating what might be called spiritual wisdom with modern Western psychology, and translating states of being traditionally understood in religious contexts into contemporary secular language.

> If we once admit that we are spiritual beings, then the whole game takes another turn. Instead of patching wrecks, or even realizing potentials, we are dismantling the barriers which are keeping us away from the divine. That which separates us from our spiritual centre has to be questioned, seen through and transformed. (Rowan 1993: 3)

Their forerunners included the American psychologist and philosopher William James (1842–1910). In the late nineteenth century James was already exploring the spiritual dimension of consciousness from a psychological perspective. In this sense, though the term was unknown to him, he anticipated some of the concerns of transpersonal psychology. *The Varieties of Religious Experience: A study in human nature* contains a series of lectures delivered at the University of Edinburgh in Scotland in 1901 and 1902. The lectures covered the nature of religion and the importance of an academic study of religion. 'James recognized the existence of a spiritual self, as well as a material and a social self. He saw it as more inner, more subjective, more dynamic' (Rowan 1993: 28).

On the basis of his own mystical experiences, James concluded that: 'there is a continuum of cosmic consciousness, against which our individuality builds but accidental fences, and into which our several minds plunge as into a mother-sea or reservoir' (Murphy and Ballou, quoted in Rowan 1993: 28). This 'mother-sea' of 'cosmic consciousness' sounds very much like Jung's collective unconscious. Along with James, transpersonal psychologists acknowledge Jung as an important influence. One of the most interesting and influential Jungian psychologists, James Hillman (1926–2011), in an open dialogue with journalist Michael Ventura, expressed an attitude of receptiveness to that aspect of the mind that is most creative, even anarchic:

> You see, Michael, for me the job of psychotherapy is to open up and deal with – no, not deal with, *encourage*, maybe even inflame – the rich and crazy mind, the wonderful aviary (the image is from Plato) of wild flying thoughts, and sex-charged fantasies, the incredible longings, bloody wounds, and the museums of archaic shards that constitute the psyche. (Hillman and Ventura 1992: 151)

Roberto Assagioli and the impulse towards self-actualization

The first psychotherapist to describe his approach as 'transpersonal' was Roberto Assagioli, an acquaintance and admirer of Jung. Assagioli (1888–1974) was born in Venice. He was introduced early to ideas from Eastern religious traditions – his mother took a close interest in Theosophy – and to music, literature and art, which would later be reflected in his expansive sense of human potential.

> It is useful to place Assagioli in his historical context. As a young medical doctor he was in his prime at the time when Einstein was developing his theory of relativity in Berne, Freud was pioneering psychoanalysis in Vienna, James Joyce was revolutionizing literature in Trieste, Jung was giving birth to analytical psychology in Zurich, Lenin was formulating the Russian revolution in Zurich, and Heidegger was preparing to espouse existentialism in Fribourg. Most of the great intellectual revolutions were initiated in central Europe

around this time, and everywhere new trends of thought were springing up. (Whitmore D. 2004: 2)

Assagioli seems to have been precocious – as a student of languages, for example, adding Greek, Latin, German and Russian to the three languages spoken in the home: Italian, French and English – and precocious also in developing his own attitudes to the new field of psychology. He studied medicine in Florence, specializing in neurology and psychiatry. By the age of 21, he had completed a doctoral dissertation. Assagioli showed great interest in Freud's work and was active in spreading the word in Florence. But he was also critical of what he saw as limitations in Freud's understanding of human nature.

The emphasis in Assigioli's thinking was on synthesis, rather than analysis. Where Freud emphasized the conflict within the psyche, with the ego pulled between superego and id, Assigioli took a more positive view of the *self* as the centre of identity. He argued that people are naturally inclined to seek self-actualization. The purpose of therapy is to enable this process and remove obstacles to it. Rejecting a Freudian model based on pathology and neurosis, he had an essentially optimistic vision of human nature and human potential. He saw the soul as the source of psychological health, believed that people need purpose and meaning in their lives, and argued that just as we suppress our baser urges, we are also inclined to quell aspects of our higher selves, such as altruism, creative inspiration, love and joy.

Assagioli corresponded with Freud, but it was with Jung, who he met while training in psychiatry in Zurich, that he felt the stronger connection. Assagioli made a distinction between Jung's collective unconscious and his notion of the transpersonal. According to Assagioli, the collective unconscious is something much wider and more inclusive, whereas the transpersonal involved individual levels of higher awareness.

In keeping with his positive outlook on human nature, Assagioli's own life seems to have been largely sunny, until he became a victim of Mussolini's fascist government. In 1938 his institute in Florence was shut down and, at the age of 50, he was arrested and endured solitary confinement for a month. A humanist, an internationalist, and a Jew, he was not viewed favourably by the fascists; nor by their Nazi allies. He spent the war years on the run.

Assagioli's model of the mind

In the 1930s Assagioli mapped his understanding of the human psyche in a diagram that, because of its oval shape, is sometimes referred to as the 'egg-diagram'. He distinguished seven areas, including three aspects of the unconscious: *lower, middle and higher*. The *lower unconscious*, like the Freudian id, is the emotionally charged realm containing complexes and fundamental drive. The *middle unconscious* is the part we can most readily tune in to, containing our current thoughts and emotions and the memories to which we have immediate access. This middle region contains within it the *field of consciousness*, at the centre of which is the *personal self*. The *higher unconscious* contains the intuitions that guide us and all our higher aspirations.

It would be tempting to map this third region onto the Freudian superego (Chapter 6), but there is a crucial difference. The superego is a somewhat oppressive presence, a kind of internalized parental voice that tends to censor and restrain. The *higher unconscious*, in contrast, is the area in which, when we gain access to it, we are most fully and creatively ourselves, experiencing moments of enlightenment and ecstasy. At the peak of this region is the *transpersonal Self*, which is the point of our purest essence, a region untouched by conscious experience. All around, touching the porous limits of the psyche, is the *collective unconscious*, a concept Assagioli drew directly from Jung.

1971 saw the founding of the Association for Transpersonal Psychology. Abraham Maslow, who had been studying peak experiences and their role in self-actualization, was a key figure in this development, along with the inspirational holocaust survivor Viktor Frankl. They were joined by the Czech psychiatrist Stanislav Grof.

Stanislav Grof and hylotropic consciousness

While working in Prague, Stanislav Grof (1931–) had characterized the particular traumas suffered by the infant at various stages of the birth process, the associated archetypal imagery, and the resulting psychological traumas that might be experienced as a result in later life. But it was his interest in what he called holotropic consciousness that established his role in this new transpersonal field. The ordinary *hylotropic* consciousness (from the Greek for 'wood' or 'matter') is concerned with the mundane level of perception that we consider our shared reality. Holotropic consciousness (from the Greek for 'whole') is characterized, in contrast, by abnormal or extraordinary states where a greater reality is glimpsed in its entirety. Such awareness might be part of a mystical experience, or might be achieved during meditation or induced with the aid of psychedelic drugs. In Czechoslovakia during the 1950s, as part of his psychoanalytic research, Grof had conducted experiments with LSD. He had also explored other techniques that departed radically from the established models of talk therapy, including the use of music and physical touch.

The exploration of the transpersonal, both in therapy and through spiritual practices, has enjoyed huge appeal for many over the past few decades. However, as psychologist and author John Rowen argues:

> It is safer and better to do our personal growth work before our spirituality, rather than leave it till later or try to avoid it altogether.

It turns out that personal growth work is not an optional extra – it is an essential step on the spiritual path. In the past, people often embarked upon the spiritual path without having done this work, and promptly fell prey to demons, devils, elementals and so forth – most of which were projections of their own shadow, their own nastiness. By going the way of counselling, therapy, group work or whatever, we dispose of all these mistakes and confusions before we start; and hence, when we meet a demon, we know exactly how to handle it and how to speak to it, without giving it a status it does not deserve. (Rowan 1976: 167)

Implications for coaching

In the field of coaching, working with reasonably healthy individuals to create a life that is more fully lived brings the coach into direct relationship with humanistic and transpersonal psychology and the possibility of helping to create a more holistic, spiritually expansive life for one's client. Exciting as these possibilities are, however, Rowan's words can be taken as a caution to coaches to keep their feet on the ground.

Humanistic principles

1. Establish collaboration with your client, based on mutual trust and respect.
2. Practise empathetic listening.
3. Communicate to the client that she has the knowledge, emotional strength and personal power to make the changes she desires.
4. Offer your client unconditional positive regard.
5. Be authentic. Who you are, as a loving, insightful person, is critical in a good coaching relationship.
6. Remember that studies show that the connection with the client turns out to be more important than which particular school or technique of coaching you adopt.
7. If appropriate, introduce your client to Maslow's Hierarchy of Needs to help her understand herself in terms of needs, desires and aspirations.
8. Discuss the phenomena of peak experiences and self-actualization with your client. She may have experienced these states, but not known how to give a name to them or understand them in a wider context.

9. A simple peak experience exercise (J. Rogers, *Coaching Skills*: 116). Ask your client:

    1. What made this moment or time special?
    2. Who else was present or involved?
    3. What were they doing?
    4. What was it that you specifically did that made it so important?
    5. What were your feelings then?

10. Above all, let your client know how much you value her as a human being and how important it is that she value herself.

Transpersonal principles

Today, increasingly, the practices inspired by transpersonal psychology are being applied in a coaching context. As people grow in maturity, they often feel the need to find a deeper meaning, including a sense of transcendence, expressing a desire to live more fulfilling and ecstatic lives. As coaches, we might be called on to work with clients in search of more transcendent ways of living and working. Aspects of this search might include:

1. A curiosity about the transpersonal dimension of existence.
2. An understanding of what it means to experience life in a more transcendent fashion.
3. An awareness of flow, peak moments and experiences of ecstasy.
4. An understanding of the power we all have to create an extraordinary experience for ourselves, despite external circumstances.
5. An openness to greater spiritual awareness.
6. An identification with all persons and all living things.
7. An experience of life beyond time and space.

These experiences are not ones that can be 'coached', but they might arise out of coaching work that helps a client improve her self-esteem, increases her ability to operate at higher levels of awareness, and nurtures a capacity for deeper empathy.

Chapter 10: Strategies for change: CBT and TA

Cognitive behavioural coaching is an evidence-based approach drawn from the theories of Beck and Ellis. It has been described as an integrative approach, which combines the use of cognitive, imaginal, behavioural, problem-solving and solution-seeking techniques and strategies within a cognitive-behavioural framework. The main premise is that how we tackle a particular task or event is largely, although not completely, determined by our perceptions and beliefs about it.

Using a collaborative interpersonal coaching style, I help coachees understand how they can enhance their performance and achieve their realistic goals by examining their thinking and developing desired behaviours. Some coachees experience goal-blocking emotions, such as anxiety, which interfere with their performance and in some cases can lead to avoidance of important tasks. I facilitate the process so that they can modify such stress-inducing thoughts, and thereby reduce performance anxiety.

I apply cognitive behavioural coaching to a wide range of contexts, including life and personal coaching, skills and performance, executive and leadership, developmental coaching, peer coaching, team coaching, career coaching, self-esteem and self-acceptance, and health and wellness coaching.

Professor Stephen Palmer
Borehamwood, United Kingdom
Centre for Coaching
International Academy for Professional Development Ltd
http://www.iafpd.com

For me, *transactional analysis* (TA) is the often-unsung hero of coaching. So much about it mirrors my own core values as a coach: for instance, the insistence on openness and equality between practitioner and client, the importance of feelings, the emphasis on autonomy and getting free of defensive thinking. More explicitly, I sometimes teach the essential TA Ego States framework to clients as a simple way of explaining glitches in relationships that might otherwise remain inexplicable. The TA concept of 'the stroke economy' is a brilliant way of understanding why so many executive clients find giving and receiving feedback so difficult.

But at the heart of the usefulness of TA is the whole idea of resisting necessary change through either self-sabotaging games playing, or what TA calls 'discounting': discounting the plain truth of evidence; discounting our own need and ability to change. TA stresses that there is always a pay-off for staying stuck, so even if staying stuck creates misery, at least the misery is familiar. Asking a client the uncomfortable question, 'So what's the pay-off here?' has often created a route to much-desired change on their part.

And every time I challenge a trainee coach who asks the question, 'How did that make you feel?', I point out, thanks to TA, that no one can make anyone feel anything. Yes, it's a choice: the ultimate foundation principle of coaching, emphasizing the responsibility each of us has to make our own choices and not to blame others when we have made a bad one.

Jenny Rogers
London, United Kingdom
Jenny Rogers Coaching
jenny@jennyrogerscoaching.com
http://www.jennyrogerscoaching.com

The principles of both transactional analysis and cognitive behavioural therapy have added significantly to professional coaching practice. Both provide tools that can help move the client towards a deeper personal understanding and a greater ability to make personal and professional life changes. TA begins with the Freudian idea of influence in early childhood; CBT has its roots in behaviourism. Both shift the emphasis towards the cognitive. They represent two very different, but important contributions, to the practice of coaching.

Cognitive behavioural therapy

There is nothing either good or bad, but thinking makes it so.

Hamlet

Watson and Skinner: behaviourism

In 1913, the American psychologist John Watson was arguing that psychology should be considered an experimental branch of natural science, and that it should aim for the same level of objectivity as other sciences, not concerning itself with introspection but only with observable behaviour. In an experiment that, these days, wouldn't get past any university ethics committee, he conditioned a child, known as Little Albert, to be frightened of a white rat by making loud clanging noises whenever the rat appeared. In 1920s Russia, the physiologist Ivan Pavlov demonstrated that dogs who were served food whenever a bell was rung would begin to salivate at the sound of the bell whether food appeared or not. He called this a conditioned stimulus response.

In the 1930s and 1940s, B. F. Skinner, an American behaviourist, shifted the emphasis from the stimulus that precedes the behaviour to the reinforcement it receives afterwards. A reward in the form of a good outcome he called positive feedback, a reward in a negative form – something bad avoided, such as not getting wet as a result of putting up an umbrella – he called negative feedback. These ideas gave rise to behaviour therapy, which was popular in the 1950s, as a way of modifying behaviour without delving into the murky territory of the mind.

Albert Ellis: rational behavioural therapy

The psychologist Albert Ellis (1913–2007) found this approach too limiting. Rather than focusing on the environment as the key factor in learning, he was interested in the way the brain processes information. The behaviourists sought to change behaviour directly, and assumed that a change in thinking would follow. Ellis wanted to help people with emotional and behavioural problems to shift both their thinking and actions concurrently.

Long before developing these theories Ellis had begun exploring ways of overcoming his own phobias and dysfunctional behaviours. As a child he had suffered emotional and physical neglect. He took responsibility for the care of his younger brother and sister, helping them get ready for school while his mother was still in bed. He spent significant periods of time in hospital with kidney disease and infections, with very few visits from his parents. He grew up extremely shy, afraid of speaking in public and with no confidence around women. At 19, in order to overcome his fear of rejection, he set himself the task, over the course of a month, of approaching 100 women in the Bronx Botanical Gardens. It was an example of what would later be recognized as a CBT experiment.

The influences of Alfred Adler and Eric Fromm, among others, and his own misgivings about psychoanalysis helped to move Ellis away from the traditional psychoanalytic model. By 1954, he had broken with psychoanalysis and he began calling himself a rational therapist.

By the mid-50s he was calling his approach Rational Emotive Behaviour Therapy. His emphasis on the interrelated importance of cognition, emotion and behaviour brought him into conflict not only with the behaviourists, who were the dominant force in experimental psychology, but also with the Freudians, who still held sway in clinical practice. Only the followers of Adler were sympathetic.

Ellis developed a list of ten specific thoughts which he called irrational ideas (Ellis and Harper, quoted in Peltier 2010: 125). Rigid and thoughtless adherence to these ideas causes people problems:

1. It is a dire necessity for an adult to be loved or approved of by almost everyone for virtually everything he or she does.
2. One should be thoroughly competent, adequate and achieving in all possible respects.
3. Certain people are bad, wicked, or villainous and they should be severely blamed and punished for their sins.
4. It is terrible, horrible and catastrophic when things are not going the way one would like them to go.
5. Human happiness is externally caused and people have little or no ability to control their sorrows or rid themselves of their negative feelings.
6. If something is, or may be, dangerous or fearsome, one should be terribly occupied with it and upset about it.
7. It is easier to avoid facing many life difficulties and self-responsibilities than to undertake more rewarding forms of self-discipline.
8. The past is all-important and because something once strongly affected one's life it should indefinitely do so.
9. People and things should be different from the way they are, and it is catastrophic if perfect solutions to the grim realities of life are not immediately found.
10. Maximum human happiness can be achieved by inertia and inaction or by passively 'enjoying oneself'.

Aaron Beck: cognitive behavioural therapy

The psychologist Aaron Beck (1921–) is credited with shaping Ellis's ideas, in the 1960s, into what is known today as cognitive behavioural therapy (CBT). Beck worked with patients, studying the relationship between their problematic behaviours and their destructive thought patterns:

> For a good part of their waking life, people monitor their thoughts, wishes, feelings and actions. Sometimes there is an internal debate as the individual weighs alternative courses of action and makes

decisions . . . Cognitive therapy consists of all the approaches that alleviate psychological distress through the medium of correcting faulty conceptions and self-signals . . . By correcting erroneous beliefs, we can damp down or alter excessive, inappropriate emotional reactions. (Beck 1976: 214)

Like the humanists and practitioners of transactional analysis, Ellis and Beck sought to bring therapeutic practices into the here and now, and develop a democratic style, where client and therapist are working together in the therapeutic engagement.

CBT is now a general term used to describe a range of therapies designed to solve problems of dysfunctional emotions, behaviours and thoughts. Common to all of them is a systematic, goal-oriented process.

Beck likened CBT to a scientific investigation. Therapist and client work together to uncover unproductive belief systems. They then view a client's belief as a hypothesis and develop experiments to test and challenge this hypothesis empirically. Once a test has been completed, therapist and client evaluate the results to determine whether the experiment has altered the client's original assumption. Other CBT activities include making lists of destructive and constructive behaviours, selecting a behaviour that needs changing, and monitoring the progress of change. Clinicians often set 'homework' so that the client is actively continuing the process between sessions.

David Burns: popular adaptations of CBT

The notion of irrational thoughts and distorted thinking are central to CBT. David Burns, a student of Beck's and the author of *Feeling Good: The New Mood Therapy* and *The Feeling Good Handbook*, has elaborated on these principles to create the 'Ten Forms of Twisted Thinking'. Burns' list, together with his descriptions, is widely available (Burns 1999: 8–11). Here are his categories freshly explained and illustrated:

1. *All-or-nothing thinking:* You see everything in black or white terms. You slip on your diet and therefore binge for the rest of the day. You don't study enough for an exam, so you skip the exam altogether. You make a rude comment to your boss, so you quit coming to work.
2. *Overgeneralization:* One piece of bad luck or a negative incident and you decide that life is always difficult. A man you meet doesn't call you, so you decide that you will never get a date. Your son gets detention after school, so you decide that he's always screwing up. Your direct report doesn't turn in an assignment on time, so you conclude she will never be a capable employee.

3. *Mental filter:* You dwell, even obsess, on the negative aspect of every situation, and ignore any hopeful signs or encouragement. Your boss offers some constructive criticism and you can't let go of the bad feeling it has created. Your child has a tantrum and you are depressed about his behaviour for days.

4. *Discounting the positive:* You have an inability to accept positive feedback. You discount praise you have received from your boss or your friends. Your husband says you look pretty, but you don't believe him – he's just your husband. Your boss pays you a compliment, but you are sure that your work wasn't that exceptional.

5. *Jumping to conclusions:* You are *sure* things will turn out badly. The car doesn't start immediately, so you assume there is something radically wrong with it. You don't hear back immediately from your doctor about a procedure, so you assume there is something terribly wrong with you. You anticipate that you will do badly on a test, even though you have studied and are prepared.

6. *Magnification:* You exaggerate your negative qualities while ignoring your positive ones. You decide that, being a bit overweight, you can't go out with your friends. You do very well in most subjects, but dwell on the one subject in which your work is average. You are sure that you will never get married because no one would want you.

7. *Emotional reasoning:* Your negative emotions cloud your objectivity. You decide that all air travel must be dangerous because you are afraid to fly on an aeroplane. You feel depressed, so you are sure that you will be depressed for the rest of your life. You are hurt by your sister, so you conclude that you are a person not worth being friends with.

8. *'Should' statements:* These are killers. They are injunctions usually from childhood. You *should* be a better person, kinder to your parents and siblings. You *should* be more outgoing at work. You *must* make sure your house is always clean. You *have to* work hard to be a good person and be loved. You *ought* to be more patient with your children.

9. *Labelling:* Like the 'all or nothing' feeling, labelling is when you decide that your identity rests on negative labels. You are a failure. You are a bad mother. You are a loser at your job. These are extreme statements which signify self-hatred, frustration and low self-esteem. You can also end up labelling others, using the same logic. Your colleague is a witch. Your next door neighbour is a fool. Your children are useless. This extreme form of categorization is detrimental to both you and those you label.

10. *Personalization:* This is a way of thinking where you hold yourself personally responsible for most events in your life – even when these events are caused by circumstances or situations not of your making.

> Your child comes home with bad grades and you conclude that you
> are a bad mother. Your spouse seems preoccupied and distant, so you
> conclude that you are a lousy wife and lover. You can also personalize
> blame on others. You decide that the reason you can't get along well
> at work is because your boss is a jerk. Your friends don't ask you to
> spend time with them, so they are all losers.

One of the most interesting aspects of CBT is the degree to which it fits into
what we call a coaching engagement. In fact, there is a current method
called Cognitive Behavioural Coaching (CBC). All forms of CBT, like coaching
engagements, are time limited. Both practices focus on the present. Both
are oriented to changing thinking, behaviour and emotions. Finally, both
practices are based on a relationship of collaboration between practitioner
and client.

Whether the process is CBC, somatic or Rogerian, or follows a more
eclectic path, recent meta-studies in therapist–client relations (Prochaska
et al. 1992) have shown that the most important factor leading to change in a
client's behaviour, irrespective of which model or school the therapist or
coach is following, is the quality of the relationship. These findings give
support to a diverse approach to coaching in which the coach feels able to
draw on a wide range of strategies and techniques according to circumstances
and the needs of the client.

Transactional analysis

> And now good morrow to our waking soules,
> Which watch not one another out of feare.

John Donne

The early life of Eric Berne

Eric Leonard Bernstein (1910–1970) was born in Montreal, Canada. He
changed his name to Eric Berne in his thirties while he was serving in the US
Army Medical Corps, having taken American citizenship. After the war he
studied under the developmental psychologist, Eric Erikson, in San Francisco.
Erikson had extended Freud's stages of childhood development into adult life,
adding four new stages. Berne was influenced by this focus on adult development. But the conceptual seeds that would grow into transactional analysis
were sown earlier in his life.

He was raised in a secure and loving family. His mother, an immigrant
from Belarus who worked as a writer and editor, encouraged him in his writing

and reading. His father was a physician who served the poor and immigrant communities in Montreal. Dr Bernstein agitated within the profession for the social problems of these patients to be addressed as well their physical symptoms, but as a young doctor of no particular status, and a Jew among Protestants, he made little headway (Berne 2010: 11–12).

Sometimes Eric would accompany his father on his rounds and was confronted early with poverty and disease and the relative privilege of his own life:

> [T]he children had coughs and runny noses and ugly outbreaks on their skins. I knew the names of ringworm and lice, and measles, mumps, and scarlet fever; the worst was diphtheria. This dirty street was their world, and I knew it was a world of germs and hunger, where I didn't belong and would not be equally received. (Berne 2010: 18)

The death of his father, when Berne was 10 and his sister Grace was 7, threw him prematurely into certain kinds of adult responsibility:

> Uncle Ike and some other men handed me a prayer book and explained that I would have to learn a prayer and say it every day for a year at the synagogue. I couldn't read the Hebrew very well, I had studied it a little from books Grandpa had given me, but there was a transliteration in English and I learned that. Then they took me to stand beside the coffin and recite the prayer with them. *Yisgadal Veyiskadash.* Take one step back at the end. I was not yet eleven years old. (Berne 2010: 97)

He had great admiration for the Rector of his school, who loved and supported him, allowing him to stay on even though he had discovered that Eric lived outside the school district. He recognized the Rector as a *menschenkenner*, a knower of people. 'Freud himself', he remarks, 'despite all his knowledge of the psychic machinery, was no *menschenkenner*, and his disciples didn't require this kind of wisdom in themselves; knowledge, perhaps, but not wisdom' (Berne 2010: 140).

His account of the end of his schooldays contains themes that are central to transactional analysis. The focus is on all those aspects of his character, whether innate or internalized during childhood under adult influence, that link him with the rest of humanity:

> So there I was, a direct descendant of Adam and Eve, facing the world at seventeen. I had few material things and no spending money . . . The most important things I owned were in my head. First, all the

things that had been put there by my parents and teachers, by books and by friends: freedoms and duties, aspirations and prohibitions. Second, all the knowledge of the world and its ways, and of the things it had to offer and could take away. Third, all the memories and desires that had grown in me since birth, all the hopes and ideals and strivings and creations that welled up from my youthful soul. (Berne 2010: 145)

Transactional analysis emerged as a popular form of psychology in the mid-60s with the publication of Berne's book, *Games People Play*. This was followed by *I'm OK, You're OK*, written by Berne's colleague, Thomas Harris, MD (1910–1995). Both books are highly readable, useful resources for the average person as well as the practitioner.

Three ego states

Transactional analysis, as a philosophy and a therapeutic methodology, is based on Freudian concepts, but it shifts the emphasis from the internal dynamics, which are the focus of psychoanalysis, to the transactions between people.

TA rests on several assumptions. First, people are OK. You're OK and I'm OK. I might not always like what you do, but I accept what you are. We are equals, regardless of status or any other human divisions. Second, everyone (except the severely brain damaged) has the capacity to think. You are responsible for yourself, and you live with the consequences of what you have decided. Third, you can decide to change. No matter what circumstances you were born into, you are not doomed to live out these circumstances. Fourth, the client practitioner relationship is one that is based on equality. Fifth, there is open, transparent communication between client and practitioner. The client is taught the elements of TA and is able to view the practitioner's notes at any point in the process. Finally, the aim of the process is for the client to achieve autonomy through consciously choosing clarity, openly sharing feelings, and getting free of defensive thinking developed in childhood.

Berne describes three ego states: the Parent, the Adult, and the Child. This division is fundamental to Transactional analysis. These states usually occur one at a time. As adults, we may inhabit any one of these three states at any moment. The Parent is the state we were taught as children by our parents and teachers and which we took on in adulthood. It is characterized by guilt, control, nurturing behaviour and 'shoulds'. The Adult is the most mature ego state, characterized by logic and reason. The Child state exists when we replay behaviours and feelings from childhood, or when we experience strong emotions and desires, such as joy, delight, fear, anger and sexual arousal.

Unhealthy childhood experiences can lead individuals to being pathologically fixated in the Child and Parent ego states.

The transactions Berne identified, which give the name to his theory, represent interactions between people. In complementary transactions, needs are expressed and met, such as problem solving (Adult to Adult) or in mutual play (Child to Child or Parent to Child). Problems arise when cross transactions occur and an Adult question is responded to with a Parent or Child response.

Four life positions

Life positions are convictions we create about ourselves which have long lasting impact. Harris describes four overarching life positions:

1. *I'm not OK – You're OK:* This is the conclusion every child arrives at, in his attempt to make sense of the world and to understand himself in relation to his parents. It affects everything he does. Because it is a *decision*, it can be overruled by a new decision, once it has been recognized. It shows up in adulthood in a tendency to compensate for a feeling of inadequacy by accumulating honours, possessions and money. This person might overwork, or might attach himself to people who lend him some of their own power and glamour.
2. *I'm Not OK – You're Not OK:* The person in this frame of mind has no hope and is likely to withdraw from other people. Whatever events in his life made him experience himself as victim, the result is that he believes he is a failure, and he will be proved right.
3. *I'm OK – You're Not OK:* Given enough brutal treatment by his parents or whoever raises him, this person will eventually conclude they're not OK and come to rely solely on himself and survive by being tough. Others will probably find him overbearing, aggressive and insensitive.
4. *I'm OK – You're OK:* This is the desired state for all adults. You regard others as equals, and you assume your life will be successful as defined by you, not by them. You can give and receive feedback without becoming defensive or aggressive. Your vulnerability, your willingness to be open to others, is a sign of your strength and self-confidence. As a conscious state, it allows room for information about other people's reality and larger conceptions of life's possibilities.

In practice, most of us are likely to adopt all four positions, if only briefly, during a typical day, but usually there's one that we're more attached to, which is our default position.

The games we play

When Berne first wrote on transactional analysis, he defined the behaviours involved in the process as 'games'. According to Berne, games are 'an ongoing series of complementary ulterior transactions progressing to a well-defined, predictable outcome. Descriptively it is a recurring set of transactions, often repetitious . . .' (Berne 1968: 48). The games we play include *Wooden Leg* (I remain attached to a handicap as an exuse for my lack of success and, if it's removed, replace it with another), *See what You Made Me Do* (I find someone else to blame when something goes wrong in my life) and *I'm Only Trying To Help You* (compulsively driven to help people, I feel hurt when my efforts are rejected).

In an article published in 1968 psychotherapist Stephen Karpman, who worked with Berne and Harris in San Francisco, described a process called the *Drama Triangle*. In the *Drama Triangle*, there are three roles: victim, persecutor, and rescuer. In common with other games, the *Drama Triangle* invariably involves a switch. The victim may turn on the persecutor, and thus take over the role of persecutor. The persecutor may turn on the rescuer ('This is none of your business'), turning the rescuer into the victim. There are no winners in the *Drama Triangle*. In fact, it is common for people who typically play persecutor and rescuer to say they feel like victims themselves.

Other key terms

1. *Transactions:* Any interaction between two people is a transaction. It might be a complementary transaction, occurring between two people in Adult mode. Or it might be problematic, occurring between, say, an Adult and a Parent.
2. *Strokes:* Strokes are units of recognition. They can be verbal or non-verbal, positive or negative. According to Berne and Harris, we live in a world that gives far too few strokes. The fact that strokes are in short supply gives rise to what they call a stroke economy. The unwritten rule, particularly for Adults, is that one shouldn't ask for strokes. Restricting strokes is a way to control others.
3. *Life Scripts:* A Life Script is the story we create about ourselves in which we are the central character. It is an unconscious decision we made early on in our life. Our life script is often a distortion of reality. It represents magical thinking. To the extent that we can consciously redefine our life script, we free ourselves from depression, longing, and feelings of things being 'less than' we'd like them to be.
4. *Injunctions:* TA identifies 12 basic injunctions about how *not* to be. Most probably, they are messages that came from childhood, and include admonitions such as *Don't be who you are, Don't change, Don't be a child, Don't grow up, Don't make it in your life, Don't think, Don't be*

close and *Don't feel.* As in other TA processes, the first task is to identify the injunctions you received before you can work on changing them.

5. *Counter-injunctions:* These are the 'do' messages we received in childhood. They have the force of superstition: you are only OK if . . . The five most powerful counter-injunctions, according to the theory, include: *Be perfect* (demanding perfection of ourselves and often those around us); *Be strong* (remain calm, controlled, which means we may stand apart from certain activities, fearing we'll look stupid); *Try hard* (the injunction of almost every conscientious parent); *Please others* (do whatever is necessary to please the people that matter and worry about changing our behaviour in case others won't like us); *Hurry up* (an injunction that often results in impatience with ourselves and with others).

6. *Discounting:* Our perceptions can be distorted in various ways, and the distortions occur beyond our conscious awareness. Discounting is the way we deny reality. The greater the perceived threat, the more fiercely we cling to the discount. We may discount: the existence of a problem; the significance of the problem; that the problem is solvable; or that we are capable of changing. The process of discounting is central to transactional analysis because it is in this process that individuals define their reality and their reasons for not changing. The misery one feels may be unbearable, but at least it's familiar.

The particular contribution of TA

This shifting division of individuals into pre-existing roles, along with the basic ego states of Parent, Adult and Child, might suggest a connection with the archetypes that inhabit the collective unconscious in Jung's model. In general, Jungians have a much more positive understanding of archetypes, seeing them as necessary guides in the unfolding narrative of life, and are less interested in making value judgements about them. Carol Pearson, in her book *Awakening the Heroes Within* (1991), identified 12 archetypes: the Innocent, the Orphan, the Warrior, the Caregiver, the Seeker, the Destroyer, the Lover, the Ruler, the Magician, the Sage, the Fool and the Creator.

> Each archetype that comes into our lives brings with it a task, a lesson, and ultimately a gift. The archetypes together teach us how to live. And the best part about it is that all the archetypes reside in each of us. That means we all have this full human potential within ourselves. (Pearson 1991: 7)

In contrast, the emphasis in TA is on correcting dysfunctional behaviours. Its brilliance is in creating a language and a set of narratives for identifying the various ways in which we create and encounter friction in our dealings with others, and presenting them in terms the general reader can understand. Thomas Harris was clear that this was his purpose:

> During the past twenty-five years, beginning with particular intensity in the years immediately following World War II, the popularity of psychiatry would seem to have created expectancies far beyond our capacity to fulfil them. Continual outpourings of psychological literature, whether printed in psychiatric journals or the *Reader's Digest*, have increased this expectancy yearly, but the chasm between this and cure seems to have widened. The question has always been how to get Freud off the couch and to the masses. (Harris 1969: xxi)

The influence of TA showed up in *est* and in the trainings that derived from *est* (Chapter 4). The Landmark exercise, in which participants are asked to separate the painful event from the story they have constructed around it, links directly with the process of identifying the injunctions, counter-injunctions and discounting behaviours internalized in childhood. With its sophisticated psychological understanding of human behaviour, TA made an important contribution to both psychotherapy and, later, to coaching. Transactional analysis followed Rogerian person-centred therapy in being deeply democratic and interactive. In addition, Berne and Harris found a language and what might be called, in the most positive sense, a mythology, to bring psychological concepts to a mass audience. This was its revolutionary contribution.

Implications for coaching

CBT

1. CBT offers useful techniques for coaching because it focuses primarily on behaviour change.
2. It can be helpful to a client, in the process of behaviour change, to have her measure and record her progress.
3. Burns' popularization of CBT has a lot to offer the coach. In particular, his list of cognitive distortions can help you understand how your client might be undermining herself. If appropriate, introduce your client to this list.
4. CBT makes us particularly alert to the interconnections between changes in thinking and changes in behaviour. A change in one can

initiate or reinforce a change in the other. In this way, our coaching can encourage upward spirals of progress.

5. CBT can be particularly useful as a coaching method when a client has difficulty self-reflecting.

TA

1. Be aware of the different ego states present in a coaching situation – both in yourself and in the client. For example, when a client is upset and angry about something that has happened to her, be aware that she is likely to be replaying the Adapted Child.

2. Remember that people are often 'stroke starved'. Our strokes to our clients are important.

3. When you hear a client's account of her early life, be conscious that you are hearing a script.

4. With your client's consent, explain the four life positions and ask the client which quadrant most accurately describes her position.

5. Notice when your client discounts a problem.

Part 3
The self and others

Then began I to dream a marvellous dream,
That I was in a wilderness I know not where.
As I looked to the east right into the sun,
I saw a tower on a hill worthily built;
A fair field full of folk found I in between,
Of all manner of men, the rich and the poor,
Working and wandering as the world asketh.

William Langland: *The Vision Concerning Piers Plowman*

It is no measure of health to be well adjusted to a profoundly sick society.

Krishnamurti

Chapter 11: We are not alone: the self, family and society

Coaching a team is very different from coaching an individual. For a start, the issues covered tend to be collective – either an issue for the team as a whole (say an external threat or opportunity), or an issue within the team as a whole (say, conflict between subgroups of the team). Another difference relates to confidentiality – what a team member might say in a one-to-one conversation can be very different to what they will say to the whole team. And a third major difference is that people come to conclusions at very different speeds. In one-to-one coaching the coach can adjust pace to the individual; in team coaching they must mediate the pace so as not to lose either the fast or the slow decision makers.

In my team coaching I find I have to pay constant attention to the duality of individual and collective needs. I also try never to lose sight of the aim of team coaching. It is not primarily about resolving a specific, current issue. It is about helping the team develop collective competence to manage issues on their own – i.e. about making the team coach obsolete as quickly as possible. So, for example, if there is an issue of conflict, the team needs to acquire tools, behaviours and ways of thinking that will allow them to transform potentially damaging conflict into positive, creative conflict.

Professor David Clutterbuck
Maidenhead, United Kingdom
Email: david@davidclutterbuckpartnership.com
Website: http://www.davidclutterbuckpartnership.com

The individual and social pressure

Nothing is bleaker than the sight of a person striving yet not fully able to control his own behaviour in a situation of consequence to him. (Milgram 1969: xiii)

Stanley Milgram's experiment

In July 1961, the Cold War was at its height. The CIA's bungled Bay of Pigs invasion of Cuba was a few months in the past; the Cuban missile crisis a year in the future. In Jerusalem the trial of the Nazi war criminal Adolf Eichmann was in progress. In New Haven, Connecticut, an advertisement appeared in a local newspaper (Milgram 1969: 14):

WE WILL PAY YOU $4.00 FOR ONE HOUR OF YOUR TIME

Persons needed for a study of memory

We will pay five hundred New Haven men to help us complete a scientific study of memory and learning . . . We need you for only one hour: there are no further obligations . . .

Please fill out the coupon below and mail it now to Professor Stanley Milgram, Department of Pyschology, Yale University

No special training, education or experience is needed

This was to become one of the most famous, controversial and illuminating experiments in the history of social science. Although the volunteers were led to believe that its purpose was to study memory, Stanley Milgram's real interest was in whether ordinary law-abiding citizens might be induced to inflict pain on an innocent victim, even to the point of death, if instructed to do so by a figure of authority.

In *Obedience to Authority*, Milgram describes 18 versions of the same experiment. In its classic form, two volunteers arrive at the laboratory at the same time. Only one of them is a genuine volunteer; he is also, without knowing it, the true subject of the experiment. The other is an accomplice, chosen for his harmless, mild-mannered appearance. The experimenter, wearing a grey technician's coat and with an air of authority, explains that the experiment is about whether people learn better if they're punished for getting things wrong. The two men are allocated roles, apparently at random, but the subject is always the 'teacher' and the accomplice always the 'learner'. They are taken to the room where the learner will apparently sit, strapped in a chair with an electrode attached to his wrist, and the teacher is given a sample electric shock of 45 volts so that he knows the nature of the punishment he will be asked to inflict.

Once the learner has been installed in his 'electric chair', the teacher is taken to an adjacent room. Communicating with the learner through a microphone, and under the watching eye of the experimenter, he is required to conduct simple memory tests, with a multiple choice structure so that the learner can respond by pressing buttons. Any mistake or failure to answer is to be punished with an electric shock. After each punishment the shock must be increased by 15 volts on a clearly labelled dial that runs from 15 to 450 volts. The higher settings carry warnings of severe danger.

Authority obeyed

Experiments in social science are often criticized for telling us things we know already. *'Girls talk about their feelings more than boys do* – and we needed a team of academics to tell us this?' Milgram forestalled any such reaction to his experiment by asking people in advance what they thought the results would be. He surveyed audiences at his lectures – psychiatrists, academics and members of the public. Their predictions were consistent, and startlingly wrong. The psychiatrists were marginally more optimistic than the others, believing that few subjects would go beyond 150 volts, and only one in a thousand would reach the full 450 volts.

In fact a pilot exercise, in which the subjects knew nothing of the learner's response except for the 'answer' lights, resulted in so many of them administering the severest punishment without objecting, that Milgram found the range of responses too limited. After that, the learner, following a fixed protocol, shouted in pain, pleaded for the experiment to stop, screamed in agony, and finally, a few steps short of the full voltage, fell silent. Even so, 68% of the subjects turned the dial to its highest setting, though almost all of them objected at various stages along the way and showed signs of stress and discomfort.

Throughout the experiment, the lab-coated experimenter, like the learner, stuck to a script, using a sequence of stock phrases to bring a resisting subject back on track: 'Please continue . . . The experiment requires that you continue . . .' (Milgram 1969: 21).

Subsequent variations put the learner in the same room as the teacher, or had a team of three teachers, two of whom were accomplices scripted to stop cooperating at predetermined stages. Interestingly, peer pressure proved a much more effective antidote to the voice of authority than the proximity of the suffering victim. In one variation, the subjects were female. Milgram noted that women tended to express themselves in more compassionate terms and exhibited higher levels of stress, but the results were the same. One observation, both paradoxical and poignant, was that subjects who had inflicted extreme punishment sometimes justified themselves afterwards by saying that they had disapproved all along of what they had been asked to do. The experiment was later repeated at several universities with thousands of participants, and Milgram's findings were broadly confirmed.

In Milgram's view, 'It is the extreme willingness of adults to go to almost any lengths on the command of an authority that constitutes the chief finding of the study and the fact most urgently demanding explanation' (Milgram 1969: 5). He suggests that the complexity of the social system separates decisions from their consequences:

> There is a fragmentation of the total human act; no one man decides to carry out the evil act and is confronted with its consequences. The person who assumes full responsibility for the act has evaporated. Perhaps this is the most common characteristic of socially organized evil in modern society. (Milgram 1969: 11)

Prejudice and conformity

One of Milgram's mentors, the American psychologist Gordon Allport (1897–1967), used to refer to Milgram's study as 'the Eichmann experiment'. In a world still coming to terms with the holocaust, the question of how the Nazis had risen to power in the heart of civilized Europe was of urgent concern, and no one reading Milgram's findings could overlook that connection. Allport's own work involved the interaction of personality with social situations. Studying Second World War refugees, he explored the nature and origins of prejudice. He devised a five-point scale of the manifestations of prejudice, rising from jokes and hate speech at the bottom, to extermination at the top.

Milgram was also influenced by Solomon Asch (1907–1996), who was his PhD supervisor at Harvard. Born in Warsaw, Ash had immigrated to the United States in 1920. A pioneer in social psychology, he studied the mechanisms of propaganda and indoctrination and, in one of his better known studies, investigated the extent to which social pressure from a group could cause an individual to conform, even to the point of saying something that is obviously incorrect.

The self in relation to the group

> I'm not afraid of storms,
> For I'm learning to sail my ship

Louisa May Alcott

Kurt Lewin: pioneer of social psychology

While Allport, Asch and Milgram were looking at the individual in society, and exploring the ways in which personal values and beliefs can be distorted or overridden by social pressure, Kurt Lewin was studying the behaviour of the group itself.

Lewin (1890–1947) was born Prussia in 1890. At the University of Munich he studied biology, and was involved in the socialist movement and women's rights. During the First World War he fought in the German army, until he was wounded and returned to Berlin to do a PhD in psychology. A behaviourist at first, he became increasingly interested in gestalt psychology, and was influenced by a group of Marxists at the Institute for Social Research. When Hitler came to power, Lewin travelled to London, where he met Eric Trist of the London Tavistock Clinic, and then on to the USA.

In 1946, while he was directing the Centre for Group Dynamics at MIT, he was asked to research approaches to combating religious and racial prejudices. He and his colleagues created a two-week programme during which a diverse group of participants would engage in discussion and decision making. The trainers and researchers would meet at the end of each day to share their observations. When the participants asked to join these evening discussions, and began questioning the interpretations of the observers, Lewin embraced this development. The combination of immediate, engaged experience and analytic detachment proved unexpectedly powerful. Almost by accident, the sensitivity training – or T-group – had come into being. In 1947, Lewin founded the National Training Laboratories at Bethel, Maine.

Lewin believed passionately in the value of the social sciences, and argued that the new stage of development they had reached as the result of the Second World War 'may prove to be as revolutionary as the atom bomb'. He explained the development in these terms:

> Applying cultural anthropology to modern rather than 'primitive' cultures, experimentation with groups inside and outside the laboratory, the measurement of socio-psychological aspects of large social bodies, the combination of economic, cultural and psychological fact-finding – all of these developments started before the war. But, by providing unprecedented facilities and by demanding realistic and workable solutions to scientific problems, the war has accelerated greatly the change of social sciences to a new developmental level. The scientific aspects of this development centre around three objectives: 1) Integrating social sciences; 2) Moving from the description of social bodies to dynamic problems of changing group life; 3) Developing new instruments and techniques of social research. (Lewin 1997: 188)

Lewin and group behaviour

Lewin's own work was extensive. He is responsible for the concept of the psychological 'field' or 'lifespace' within which individuals function, a concept that draws on gestalt theory. The field is made up of all the interdependent facts that influence someone's behaviour and are, in turn, influenced by it. Someone's behaviour can only be understood in the context of the field, which can be represented visually in the form of a map showing the network of influences. Any one person might occupy a variety of life spaces, such as family, work or school.

Lewin developed the theory that a group is different from, and more than the sum of, its parts. This concept had important implications for many disciplines, including group dynamics, systems theory and team behaviour. Lewin established some major concepts about how groups behave. They include:

1. *Group dynamics:* Groups cohere under two different conditions: interdependence of fate, when the members realize that their fate depends on the fate of the group as a whole; and task interdependence, when the members understand that they depend on the achievement of a shared goal.

2. *Democracy and groups:* Groups function far better with a democratic structure rather than an autocratic one.

3. *Force field analysis:* This is a technique for mapping the competing forces at work within a group. The 'driving' forces push for change and improvement; the 'restraining' forces resist and obstruct. The challenge is to raise the point of equilibrium between the two.

4. *Unfreezing:* Before change is possible, there must be motivation for change. Group members must be able to let go of cherished assumptions. Challenging a person's belief system to make change possible Lewin called 'unfreezing'.

5. *Participant observation:* Groups are more skilful when members move back and forth from participating emotionally in the group, to observing the group objectively.

Wilfred Bion and the group experience

As an officer in the Tank Corps in the final years of the First World War, Wilfred Bion (1897–1979) saw serious action. For one battle, in which he showed extraordinary courage, he was awarded the DSO. Many years later his daughter suggested that his work as an analyst might have been significantly influenced by his experience of war, where primitive thinking is likely, at any time, to swamp rational control.

Bion spent the interwar years studying history at Oxford, medicine at UCL, and psychotherapy at the Tavistock Clinic. The Second World War saw him back in uniform in the Medical Corps, where he worked with Tavistock colleagues on new treatments for post-traumatic stress disorder, known then as shell shock. After the war he went into analysis with Melanie Klein and wrote extensively about schizophrenia.

In 1961 he wrote a paper called *Experiences in Groups*, which quickly came to be considered a classic study of group dynamics. Bion had, by this stage, departed somewhat from Freudian orthodoxy, but the influence of Freud's psychodynamic thinking is clear. Drawing directly on his own experiences in a military psychiatric hospital and at the Tavistock Clinic, Bion describes the progress of various groups over which he has presided. I might have said groups he has *led*, except that Bion's stance is persistently to abdicate authority in order to throw the group back on its own resources. He quotes verbal exchanges and other developments that constitute the surface progress of the group, but his real interest is in the underlying feelings and shifting allegiances that make up the group's unconscious life. He observes particularly the various ways in which the group functions as a coherent entity; in selecting a leader, for example, or in excluding someone.

The paper often has a narrative structure rather than an analytical one, with theoretical observations interspersed along the way. One of his emerging conclusions is that, whatever its conscious task, and whatever it believes itself to be doing, the group is generally functioning according to certain basic assumptions:

1. A group wants security and is inclined to be dependent on its leader, sometimes to the point of becoming passive. Eventually, resentment at its dependency can lead to rebellion, and the replacement of the old leader with a new one.
2. Self-preservation is the group's main purpose, and it seems to know only two techniques of self-preservation – fight or flight. In fight mode, one person might be scapegoated and blamed for the group's failure. In flight mode, the group gives up on achieving anything and fills its time in avoidance activities.
3. The group will place its hope in any two people who engage with each other. The assumption here is that something is happening in this pairing, whatever the gender of the participants, that is equivalent to sex. As long as two people are interacting with any intensity, it is assumed that something creative will occur and the others need only wait in hopeful anticipation.

Bion extends a number of other Freudian concepts from the individual psyche to the group. The group might engage in *projection*, attributing its own fears, inadequacies or desires to some external agent. Or it might draw the leader into the psychic drama of *transference* and *counter-transference*, projecting positive or negative feeling onto the leader, who in turn projects his own internal reality onto the group.

The self and the system

> This is my letter to the world
> That never wrote to me

Emily Dickinson

Gregory Bateson and the schizophrenia project

Gregory Bateson (1904–1980) was the youngest of three brothers. When he was 14 his oldest brother John was killed in the First World War. Four years later, the second brother, Martin, shot himself in Piccadilly Circus on John's birthday; perhaps because of an unhappy love affair; perhaps because he was in conflict with his father over his desire to write plays and poems instead of becoming a scientist.

It's too easy to make glib connections between someone's personal experiences and the subsequent path of their life and ideas, and particularly tempting when those ideas relate so directly to the impact of the family dynamics on the individual. What motivates anyone to any kind of achievement, or inspires any particular intellectual leap, is ultimately unknowable. It's enough to observe that Gregory Bateson fulfilled the expectations of his father, the distinguished geneticist William Bateson, in becoming a scientist, but spent his most productive years analysing the environmental causes of mental illness.

Bateson initially studied biology. Then, after a period lecturing in linguistics at the University of Sydney, he became a fellow of St John's College, Cambridge. During the 1930s he was in New Guinea working as an anthropologist. He married the anthropologist Margaret Meade and travelled with her to Bali. There, he observed that Balinese mothers tend to disengage when their children express strong feelings of anger or affection, whereas Western mothers typically respond with an increased level of attention. As Bateson saw it, this disengagement has the effect of muting the interaction. The Western response, in contrast, escalates the dynamics either of rivalry, or of dominance and submission.

His interest in the mother–child relationships and the system of interconnections with families found a new outlet in the 1950s when he was studying schizophrenia in Palo Alto, California. Bateson and his colleagues, Donald Jackson, Jay Healey and John Weakland, worked with hospitalized patients and also interviewed parents and siblings, though families were not observed interacting as units.

They observed that the stability, or homeostasis, of the family is achieved by feedback that monitors and adjusts the behaviour of the family members. When the system is disturbed, it reacts to restore balance. The schizophrenic behaviour of the child might be one mechanism for achieving stability. If parents are fighting, the schizophrenic behaviour stops the conflict and unites the parents in concern for the 'patient'.

Schizophrenia remains ill-defined, and is in effect an umbrella term to cover a range of behaviours whose causes are not understood. In fact, since Bateson's work more evidence has emerged of the genetic component underlying schizophrenic symptoms. Recent research suggests that such symptoms may be caused by a retrovirus that can be inherited and lie dormant until something triggers it. But Bateson's theories are less significant as explanations of schizophrenia than for the light they shed on the way families work and for the self-balancing structures that operate in all kinds of human systems. For example, the idea that the child who 'acts out' or displays signs of disturbance may be taking on a role required by the family system has achieved widespread currency. And similar thinking has been applied to work teams and organizations.

Bateson and the double bind

In studying schizophrenics, Bateson and his colleagues also introduced the concept of the double bind. The individual, typically a child, is subjected to two contradictory demands by someone in authority, typically a parent. One injunction is made explicit and is likely to be unobjectionable (*Be self-confident. Make your own decisions. I want you to be happy . . .*). But it is contradicted by an unstated counter-injunction (*Conform to my wishes. Be smaller or less than yourself. Don't compete . . .*). As described by the family therapist Lynn Hoffman, 'A double bind was in essence a multilevel communication in which an overt demand at one level was covertly nullified or contradicted at another level' (Hoffman 1981: 20). Three conditions are necessary for conflicting injunctions to become a double bind in its classic form:

1. The 'victim' is not able to point out the contradiction, either because they can't see it themselves, or because 'meta-communication' is not allowed.
2. The 'victim' cannot leave the 'communication field'. A child, for example, has no choice but to remain a member of the family.
3. Failure to fulfil either injunction is punished, usually by the withdrawal of love.

Bateson's ideas have had a huge influence on family therapy and on systems theory more generally. In the words of Fritjof Capra:

Bateson championed a new way of thinking, which is extremely relevant to our time – thinking in terms of relationships, connections, patterns, and context. As we replace the Newtonian metaphor of the world as a machine by the metaphor of the network, and as complexity becomes the principal focus in science, the kind of systemic thinking that Bateson advocated is becoming crucial. (Capra, *Homage to Gregory Bateson*)

The self in the family

If you cannot get rid of the family skeleton, you may as well make it dance.

George Bernard Shaw, *Immaturity*

Murray Bowen and the need for differentiation

Like Gregory Bateson and the Palo Alto group, Murray Bowen (1913–1990) was at work in the 1950s observing the families of schizophrenic patients. The conclusions he drew transformed the field of family therapy. The Bowen Theory is psychodynamic in its approach, and encourages new levels of communication. It involves coaching family members to go back to their families of origin to achieve personal individuation and autonomy. For Bowen, therapy is a lifelong journey towards self-discovery that might include visiting ageing parents and other relatives to repair broken relationships.

Bowen believed that emotional illness is passed down through families. Patterns of family dysfunction can be traced back through time. To record such patterns, he developed the *genogram*, a family tree designed to diagram dysfunctional relationships across generations.

Some people are better able than others to manage their relation to their family of origin, to negotiate successfully between connection and individuality, so they don't get drawn into the drama of other people's emotions. In Bowen's terms, such people have achieved a high degree of *differentiation*. Quite different from differentiation is the experience of *emotional cut-off*, when someone responds to the stress of emotional entanglement by withdrawing. Individuals with low differentiation are likely to conform to family expectations in adulthood and to pressure others to conform to their own expectations, thus repeating the pattern of emotional *fusion*. Differentiation has an *intra-psychic* as well as an *interpersonal* dimension. According to Bowen, intra-psychic differentiation is the ability to separate feeling from thinking:

Undifferentiated people hardly distinguish thoughts from feelings; their intellects are so flooded with feelings that they are almost incapable of objective thinking. Their lives are governed by an accretion of feelings from those around them, either blindly adhered to or angrily rejected. The differentiated person, on the other hand, is not a cold fish who only thinks and never feels. Instead, he or she is able to balance thinking and feeling: capable of strong emotion and spontaneity, but also capable of the restraint and objectivity that comes with the ability to resist the pull of emotional impulses. (Nichols and Schwartz 1995: 371)

Triangles are forever

The differentiated person is more likely to resist the force of *triangulation*. Bowen is credited with establishing the triangle as the universal unit of analysis in family systems therapy. According to Bowen, the function of a triangle is to spread and shift anxiety and preserve stability within the family. A two-person emotional system under stress will pull a third person into its orbit to create a triangle. Bowen saw triangles as a permanent fact of family life:

> Triangles are forever, at least in families. Once the emotional circuitry of a triangle is in place, it usually outlives the people who participate in it. If one member of a triangle dies, another person usually replaces him. The actors come and go, but the play lives on through the generations. (Kerr and Bowen 1988: 135)

In 1967, Bowen presented a paper at a symposium in which he described his own family of origin, a large extended family going back many generations, which dominated a small southern town. The research process he used was to send letters to various relatives detailing unpleasant gossip and, in effect, revealing to the entire extended family all of the secrets and prejudices that had previously been kept intact. The letters announced an impending visit and were signed with descriptors such as 'Your Meddlesome Brother' or 'Your Strategic Son'. Bowen then showed up to deal with the anger and sense of betrayal from his family:

> The effect on the family was dramatic. It loosened up many closed-off relationships and – once the original fury against Bowen himself had died down – it created a climate of better feelings all around. The effect on the symposium was equally dramatic . . . a blow-by-blow account of his incredible journey – the first time, in the experience of most of his audience, that a practitioner had ever attempted to change and influence his own family or described such a literally 'convention-shattering' procedure to an august body of colleagues. (Hoffman 1981: 245)

Salvador Minuchin: structural family therapy

Salvador Minuchin (1913–1990) was born and raised in Argentina. As a young man he joined the Israeli army and then moved to New York. Minuchin became the Director of the Philadelphia Child Guidance Clinic, working with disadvantaged families. Drawing on ideas from general systems theory developed in the 1940s and 1950s, Minuchin and his colleagues developed the essential components of the structural model which are still taught to students of psychotherapy and widely used in therapeutic family interventions.

Structural family therapy begins with the assumption that every family has a structure and that this structure is revealed only when the family is in action. Interactions within the family follow predictable sequences, being governed by a set of rules that are mainly covert. Some of these rules are universal, and can be recognized in all families; others are idiosyncratic.

The family structure is made up of interconnecting subsystems, in which individual family members play different roles. Behaviour appropriate in one subsystem may be inappropriate in another. For example, if a mother, accustomed to scolding a child, scolds her husband in the same way, this is potentially destructive.

The therapy is designed to resolve the presenting problem by reorganizing the family structure. Typically it is a child who is identified as having a problem, but the family dysfunction often originates with the couple, who form the most powerful system.

> In treatment the focus frequently shifts from the child's symptoms to conflict between the parents. When this happens I continue to concentrate on the child's problems but expand the focus to include the marital problems – that is, I ask the spouses to look at how their conflict is being played out in the child's symptoms. Once again, we have a kaleidoscopic shift. I don't deny the child's symptoms; I don't minimize the spouses' conflict. I simply suggest that they are both part of a family grappling with difficulties and getting stuck with narrow solutions. (Minuchin 1993: 112)

Separating individuals and subsystems are invisible boundaries. The purpose of these boundaries is to manage proximity and hierarchy. If boundaries in a family are too rigid, the result is disengagement or emotional distancing on the part of certain family members. If boundaries are too weak, or diffuse, the result is enmeshment – a fusing of roles and a tendency for some family member to be overly dependent on others. Minuchin assumes that the single most important boundary in the family system is the one that separates one generation from another.

Minuchin's early work and research focused on families from inner city slums, where delinquency was common, particularly among adolescents. In this situation there is much to be said for re-establishing order within the family by strengthening the generational boundary. In different circumstances, however, an overly rigid hierarchy might be part of the problem. Minuchin has been criticized for overemphasizing the importance of hierarchy and for not being particularly sensitive to gender issues. On the other hand, he was unusually alert to the impact on families of the wider social context:

> During the late sixties and seventies, we began to explore not just family therapy but the social context in which families are embedded. This was, of course, a natural development for a systemic thinker who is continually pushed to look at connections with larger systems, but it also seemed a natural continuity in my life . . . The impact of multiple social context had shaped me, and I was aware of being different in different cultures. (Minuchin 1993: 33)

Virginia Satir: experiential family therapy

Virginia Satir (1916–1988) was the oldest of five children. From a very young age she was a curious and prolific reader. She was also an observer. As a child she sensed that 'a lot went on in families that didn't meet the eye' and, at the age of 5, decided that in adult life she would be 'a children's detective on adults'.

As a practising psychotherapist in Illinois in the mid-1950s she was actively promoting the radical idea that therapists should work with families rather than individuals. She developed the concept of the 'presenting issue' – the surface problem that was often merely the symptom of something dysfunctional in the family system.

Satir was involved with the Palo Alto group in the early 1960s, treating schizophrenic patients, but found a more appreciative home among the humanist psychologists, particularly Carl Rogers and Abraham Maslow, whom she worked with for a time at the Esalen Institute. Partly in reaction to the systemic models of theorists such as Bateson and Minuchin, she developed an experiential approach to family therapy, which put less emphasis on theoretical constructs, focusing instead on exploring the subjective experience of family members and helping them to get in touch with unexpressed or unconscious feelings and to communicate them authentically:

> In Satir's view, clarification of communication is part of what will free the psychotic from his position of understanding the buried messages and having to respond to them, yet having to deny that he understands or responds to them or that they even exist. (Hoffman 1981: 223)

She encouraged spontaneity and creativity in her clinical work, and the extended family was often included. In all this, she emphasized the importance of self-esteem. She was recognized as a particularly brilliant practitioner, who exercised enormous sensitivity and skill in unpacking the dysfunction at the heart of the family system and exposing discrepancies in communication, while validating the experience of every individual:

> Satir was the prototypical nurturing therapist in a field enamoured with experience-distance concepts and tricky strategic manoeuvres. Her warmth and genuineness gave her a tremendous impact as she travelled all over the country leading demonstrations and workshops. Her ability to move large audiences in experimental exercises made her a legend as family therapy's most celebrated humanist. (Nichols and Schwartz 1995: 289)

In her middle years, Satir moved away from family therapy and began facilitating larger groups of people. She created the Virginia Satir Change Process model which is still used in organizational training and management today. Her books, *Conjoint Family Therapy* (1964), *Peoplemaking* (1972) and *The New Peoplemaking* (1988) became popular with the public, as well as being respected in the therapeutic community. Like Rogers and Maslow, her faith in human potential was boundless.

Implications for coaching

1. People can be influenced against their better judgement. As coaches we have a role in validating our client's thoughts and feelings, and encouraging them to trust their own values.
2. An understanding of group behaviour is important for the coach, both in the role of group facilitator and in helping an individual client.
3. Identifying what might be happening in a group (such as flight-or-fight, group dependency or pairing) can be enormously revealing – and relieving – to a client.
4. In team coaching, knowledge of group behaviour can help you design effective, democratic teams. It can also help you clarify the task a team needs to accomplish, and how the team members can best accomplish the task.
5. Knowing the double bind concept can be critical in helping clients understand their own motivation and the motivations of others.

6. The concept of triangles can help your client understand her own behaviour as well as the behaviour of a colleague or family member. Triangulation is a common method of gaining rapport with someone, at the cost of excluding a third party.

7. Minuchin's concept of boundaries can be critical in understanding human behaviour. A recent study (A. Litwin, *CGO Insights*) pointed out that women in the workplace sometimes have more trouble drawing lines between friendships and professional relationships. This blurring of boundaries can cause unnecessary conflict between individuals and make women appear less professional.

8. Without dwelling on the past, it can be important to acknowledge family relationships and behaviours that have played a role in shaping the client's personality and decisions.

9. Virginia Satir's acceptance of people as they are, and her sympathy for the human condition as it plays out within the family and in larger groups, can be an inspiration to us in our work.

Chapter 12: Identity and employment: finding ourselves in the workplace

I often invite clients struggling in workplace situations to engage in critical self-reflection so they can learn to attend to their own thoughts, feelings and actions in situations where they experience difficulty. The aim is for the client to learn something about themselves or their situation, which they didn't know before. This new knowledge enables them to generate new ideas about how to adapt their performance over time, so that they get more of the results they are looking for. Insights achieved during this kind of work may sometimes be transformative, in that the client recognizes an unhelpful belief about themselves or others, or notices a faulty assumption, which is limiting their behaviour.

The feelings which accompany such deep learning are not always comfortable and can be disorientating. Some clients may feel surprise, confusion and even shame when they notice their own theory in use – that is what they actually do in practice as opposed to what they believe they do. At the point of transformation it is critical that I can contain these emotions, even if the client doesn't like what they see. I model a non-judgemental stance so that the client can see and feel it is safe and acceptable to be less than perfect – that as one human being to another we can show compassion to ourselves and each other.

This period of disorientation is a new space full of possibilities. It is the space from which clients can generate new ideas about how to move forward in a different way, which can be developed and refined over time into a new theory. Furthermore, this new way of working is often more aligned with their values and brings with it more of a sense of ease within their own approach and their experience of their work.

Sue Burnell
Surrey, United Kingdom
Partner, Accelerated Success
sue@acceleratedsuccess.co.uk
http://www.acceleratedsuccess.co.uk

A timeless struggle

> The strongest bond of human sympathy outside the family relation
> should be one uniting working people of all nations and tongues and
> kindreds.
>
> Abraham Lincoln

Diggers, Luddites and the ownership of work

In the middle of the seventeenth century, when Oliver Cromwell was the Lord
Protector of England, there were popular uprisings by groups calling themselves
Levellers and Diggers. Reacting to the stark imbalance of wealth in England,
and to the enclosing of common land by powerful individuals, and inspired
by the revolutionary energy of the time, the Diggers attempted to redefine
work by living collectively on the land and forming institutions that fostered
the relationship of common people to the production of food.

The immediate pressures were economic. People robbed of their access
to the land went hungry. In the view of the religious reformer and political
activist Gerrard Winstanley, 'True freedom lies where a man receives his
nourishment and preservation, that is in the use of the earth ... A man
had better have no body than to have no food for it' (Hill 1975: 134). But
the ideals of the movement tapped into a deeper feeling that people
need some sense of ownership of their work, and that the alternative is a form
of slavery:

> In the beginning of time, the great creator, Reason, made the earth to
> be a common treasury ... Not one word was spoken in the beginning
> that one branch of mankind should rule over another ... But selfish
> imaginations ... did set up one man to teach and rule over another.
> And thereby ... man was brought into bondage, and became a greater
> slave to such of his own kind than the beasts of the field were to him.
> (Winstanley, quoted in Hill 1975: 132)

One hundred and fifty years later, textile artisans joined together to protest
against the mechanization of their industry. Again there was a pressing
material motive. Craftsman weavers were being pushed out of work by the
cheaper products of the new machines. But, as with the Diggers, there were
larger issues at stake. The weaver could take satisfaction in a skill acquired
over many years; he was in control of his own product; and he had a say in
his own economic destiny. Writing in the early nineteenth century,
one commentator described the vanished life of the self-employed weaver in
these idyllic terms:

> The Workshop of the weaver was a rural cottage, from which when he was tired of sedentary labour he could sally forth into his little garden, and with the spade or the hoe tend its culinary productions. The cotton wool which was to form his weft was picked clean by the fingers of his younger children, and was carded and spun by the older girls assisted by his wife, and the yarn was woven by himself assisted by his sons. (Andrew Ure, quoted in Sale 1995: 25)

In contrast, a worker in one of the new textile mills might be required to work for anything between 12 and 16 hours a day, and liable to fines for being five minutes late, for being found dirty at his work, or for whistling. In 1831, after visiting one such mill, a Leeds doctor reported:

> While the engine works, the people must work. Men, women, and children are thus yoke-fellows with iron and steam; the animal machine – fragile at best, subject to a thousand sources of suffering, and doomed, by nature in its best state, to a short-lived existence, changing every moment, and hastening to decay – is matched to an iron machine insensible to suffering and fatigue. (C. Turner Thackrah, quoted in Sale 1995: 31)

Those weavers who protested against mechanization by breaking machines were called Luddites, after a legendary machine wrecker about whom little is known except the name Ned Ludd. Sabotage and vandalism are harder to defend than the actions of the Diggers, which mainly consisted of planting carrots, parsnips and runner beans. The term Luddite has come to mean any destructive resistance to progress; any stubborn clinging to outmoded ways. As a class of elite craftsmen whose skills were fast becoming redundant, the Luddites were certainly standing against the tide. In terms of a larger economic analysis that sees industrialization as the engine of wealth, eventually, for the many as well as the few, they can be criticized for taking a narrow view. But their drama is played out wherever human skill is devalued. Luddites were on the wrong side of history, but expressed an essential human attachment to an acquired body of knowledge and technique and the right of people to control their relationship to work.

Between 1860 and 1910, the Arts and Crafts movement flourished in England, led by the artist and writer William Morris (1834–1896) and inspired by the writings of John Ruskin (1819–1900). The movement sought to re-inspire the decorative arts through hand-crafted household items, using simple forms. The desire was to produce beautiful, useful items which were not made by machines, but designed and crafted by individuals. The movement began in England, but spread to Europe and America. Its central aesthetic belief was expressed by Morris in these terms: 'Have nothing in your houses that you do not know to be useful, or believe to be beautiful.'

Studs Terkel and the voices of working people

Studs Terkel (1912–2008) was an American author, historian, actor and broadcaster. Terkel was born in New York, but moved early in his life to Chicago, where he stayed for the rest of his life. He credited his compassion for humanity to his early years spent hanging around the rooming house that his left-leaning parents ran, which also served as a meeting place for people from all walks of life. In the 1930s and 1940s he joined the Federal Writers' Project, which was run by President Roosevelt's Works Progress Administration, and worked in radio as a news commentator and disc jockey. In the 1960s, Terkel's interest in oral history led him to write a series of books based on interviews with ordinary people, including *Division Street America* (1967), in which a variety of Chicago residents – cops, cabbies, CEOs, advertising guys, nuns – talk about their lives, *Hard Times* (1970), a mosaic of recollections of the Great Depression, and *Working* (1974), which provides remarkable insights into people's attitudes to their jobs: 'Work,' Terkel tells us, 'is about a daily search for meaning as well as daily bread, for recognition as well as cash, for astonishment rather than torpor, in short for a sort of life, rather than a Monday-to-Friday sort of dying' (Terkel 2004: xiii).

Working is a dramatic and sometimes devastating look into the hearts of working people. Terkel had an exceptional gift for connecting with his interviewees and encouraging them to open up – often about the creativity they bring to mundane tasks. As he describes his interviewing process, 'The talk was idiomatic rather than academic. In short it was conversation. In time, the sluice gates of dammed up hurts and dreams were opened' (Terkel 2004: xx–xxi).

In essence the book is a series of accounts of what people do every day at work. Some of the stories are angry or bitter, bored or resigned; others are self-aggrandizing; and still others, humorous or ironic. What all of them have in common is an articulacy built on a desire to find meaning in work and derive emotional satisfaction from it.

Because *Working* was written in the 1970s, before information technology had transformed the way we do business, the kinds of occupations reported are somewhat dated. There are no call centres or other manifestations of what Simon Head has called 'The New Ruthless Economy'. But the voices of people struggling to find a meeting point between their jobs and their identities is timeless. Delores Dante, for example, has been a waitress in a fashionable restaurant for 23 years. She thinks of what she does as an art: 'When I put the plate down, you don't hear a sound. When I pick up a glass, I want it to be just right. When someone says, How come you're just a waitress? I say, "Don't you think you deserve being served by me?"' (Terkel 2004: xii). As much as our partners and our families, our jobs are what define us. Without offering an analysis or proposing policies, *Working* poignantly illustrates our shared quest for an authentic emotional connection to the work we do. In the words of

Nora Watson: 'I think most of us are looking for a calling, not a job. Most of us . . . have jobs that are too small for our spirit. Jobs are just not big enough for people' (Terkel 2004: xxiv).

Richard Sennett and the new capitalism

Richard Sennett (1943–) is an American professor of sociology who divides his time between the London School of Economics and New York University. His many books include *The Corrosion of Character: The Personal Consequences of Work in the New Capitalism* (1998). He studies the effects on the individual of new forms of employment:

> Post-Modern works seem to have two main feelings: at best a sense of risk or insecurity; at worst a sense of betrayal. The modern covenant of mutual, life-long loyalty between employers and employees is gone. So is life-long vocation or career, as people have portfolio careers and short-term contracting or 'temping' becomes permanent. High expectations get deflated as many are in jobs way below their education. Waiting tables is no longer a way to pay your way through university, but through life. Many professionals who enter, for example, medicine or law with youthful idealism, find themselves increasingly reduced to technicians and acting accountants. Others, having served employers faithfully for years, find themselves, like Willie Loman in Death of a Salesman, 'thrown away like a piece of fruit'. (Sennett: http://www.zadok.org.au/perspectives/issue63/reviews/corrosion6301.shtml)

- *The flexible working world:* Most people know that wherever they are working, it won't last for their working lifetime, and possibly not even until next year. While this has been touted as giving employees increased freedom, the result of this new work situation, Sennett argues, is an increase in anxiety among many employees.
- *Fordism:* In processes that involve technically based labour, skilled craftspeople are increasingly replaced with so-called 'specialized workers'. The result is that, just as the assembly line worker loses connection with the whole product, employees only understand their own portion of the work. This often results in depression, feelings of alienation, and a loss in productivity. In addition, the 'brainwork' and the leadership become geographically detached from the manufacturing process. Employees feel little engagement with the company as a whole, and advancement is rare.
- *Downsizing:* To save costs, companies are using a smaller number of managers and giving them control over a greater number of jobs. This is sometimes euphemistically called 're-engineering': 'Perfectly

viable businesses are gutted or abandoned, capable employees are set adrift rather than rewarded, simply because the organization must prove to the market that it is capable of change' (Sennett 1998: 51). Under these conditions, which are at an epidemic level, there is a decline in morale and motivation of all employees, and everyone is waiting for the next shoe to drop.

- *Decentralization without redistribution of power:* This results in confusion, uncertainty and anxiety. There is no longer a clear structure that defines where the power lies.
- *Flexitime:* The location of the employee's work is shifted outside the factory or business, but the employee does not gain any greater control over the process itself. In addition, work schedules are often electronically monitored: 'Workers thus exchange one form of submission to power – face to face – for another which is electronic' (Sennett 1998: 59).

During the 15 years since Sennett's work was published the economy has taken a severe hit, while the disintegration of more traditional forms of employment that Sennett describes has continued. People are increasingly thrown on their own resources of energy and enterprise. They are called upon to overcome feelings of disappointment or anxiety, and to reinvent themselves. This is a challenge at any age – for new graduates, who have invested in many years of study only to be faced by a squeezed job market, and for those unexpectedly seeking new employment at midlife, feeling betrayed by the companies they have worked for and cared about. This is the particular challenge of our time: to find the new opportunities in an inhospitable economy.

The female experience

> Self-development is a higher duty than self-sacrifice.
>
> Elizabeth Cady Stanton

Deborah Tannen and the way we talk

Deborah Tannen (1945–) is an American academic and linguistics professor. She has written extensively on ways in which gender affects conversational style. According to Tannen, in work situations, men and women have different way of communicating and derive different meanings from language:

> Conversational rituals common among men often involve using opposition such as banter, joking, teasing, and playful put-downs,

and expending effort to avoid the one-down position in the interaction. Conversational rituals common among women are often ways of maintaining an appearance of equality, taking into account the effect of the exchange on the other person, and expending effort to downplay the speaker's authority so they can get the job done without flexing their muscles in an obvious way. (Tannen 1994: 33)

Tannen describes differences in language as male–female dichotomies. Some of these include:

1. *Status versus support:* Conversation for men is often a contest, either to achieve the upper hand, or to prevent other people from pushing them around. For women, talk is more likely to be a way of expressing mutual support.
2. *Independence versus intimacy:* Women often use conversation to preserve intimacy, whereas men use it to assert their independence.
3. *Advice versus understanding:* Often women want someone to listen to their problems with understanding, whereas men are inclined to give advice and look for solutions.
4. *Orders versus proposals:* When a woman says 'Let's park over there,' a man can hear it as an order. 'Do you want to clean up now, before lunch?' can come across as an attempt to manipulate.
5. *Conflict versus compromise:* Generally, men are more comfortable with verbal conflict. Women tend not to ask directly for what they want. *She* finds *him* confrontational. *He* considers *her* manipulative.

Differences may be fine, but as Tannen notes: 'The male is seen as normative, the female as departing from the norm . . . Furthermore, if women's and men's styles are shown to be different, it is usually women who are told to change' (Tannen, quoted in Peltier 2010: 267). In workplace situations, for the most part, women have three choices: talk (and act) like your male counterparts, resign yourself to a more inferior work position, or leave the company and start your own business.

Arlie Hochschild and emotional labour

Arlie Hochschild (1940–) is a sociology professor at the University of California, Berkeley. She has written numerous books on working, including *The Managed Heart*, *The Second Shift* and *The Time Bind*. The theme that runs throughout her writing is the emotional cost of work and the attempts of working people to create a meaningful life.

In *The Managed Heart*, Hochschild interviewed flight attendants who were taught, in all circumstances, to smile. Hochschild describes this job requirement as *emotional labour*. She defines this as 'labour that requires one to induce or sustain the outward countenance that produces the proper state of mind in others – in this case a sense of being cared for in a convivial and safe place' (Hochschild 2005: 7). Hochschild finds that attendants often experience stress as a result of being unable to display authentic emotional reactions; a weariness that comes from constantly manufacturing outward signs of positive feeling in the form of smiles that are like make-up – 'on' them but not 'of' them:

> Coping with the costs of emotional labor calls for great inventiveness. Among themselves, flight attendants build up an alternative way of experiencing a smile or the word 'girl' – a way that involves anger and joking and mutual support on the job. And in their private lives – driving back home on the freeway, talking quietly with a loved one, sorting it out in the occasional intimacy of a worker-to-worker talk – they separate the company's meaning of anger from their own meaning, the company rules of feeling from their own. They try to reclaim the managed heart. (Hochschild 2005: 197)

Hochschild estimates that a third of all American workers, and a half of American women in work, have jobs that demand a degree of emotional labour.

The struggle to integrate one's personal identity with one's working life, and to find a manageable balance between work and personal life, are recurrent themes in Hochschild's writing. In *The Second Shift*, she studies the problem of women still doing the majority of household tasks, when both partners are working outside of the home. In *The Time Bind*, she explores the discrepancy between the desire of working parents to spend time with their families, and the reality that, increasingly, parents are not spending time with each other or their children.

Hochschild cites the great mid-twentieth-century sociologist C. Wright Mills as an inspiration. In *The Sociological Imagination*, Mills wrote about the need for academics to understand that any historical trend is also a story of individual men and women:

> When a society is industrialized, a peasant becomes a worker; a feudal lord is liquidated or becomes a businessman. When classes rise or fall, a man is employed or unemployed; when the rate of investment goes up or down, a man takes new heart or goes broke. When wars happen, an insurance salesman becomes a rocket launcher; a store clerk, a radar man; a wife lives alone; a child grows up without a father. Neither the life of an individual nor the history of society can be understood without understanding both. (Mills 1959: 3)

Recent research into female leadership

According to Sally Helgesen, leadership consultant, women in leadership positions display certain distinct leadership qualities that have become both needed and valued in today's world. Her research in *The Female Leadership Advantage* (1995) found the following behaviours particular to female managers:

1. Women worked at a steady pace, but with small breaks scheduled throughout the day.
2. Women did not view unscheduled tasks and encounters as interruptions. They tended to view them as part of caring, being involved, helping and being responsible.
3. Women made time for activities not directly related to their work.
4. Women maintained a complex network of relationships with people outside their organization.
5. Women saw their identities as complex and multifaceted.

Helgesen concludes that women leaders have developed skills that are multifaceted, collaborative, networked, creative and democratic. These qualities present the possibility of a qualitatively different kind of leadership style – one that is more democratic and inclusive.

Academic researchers Connie Gersick and Kathy Kram conducted an exploratory study in 2002, interviewing a small cohort of high-achieving executive women ages 45 to 55 from the financial services industry. The authors were interested in the patterns of individuals' lives over the whole life course. Specific findings from Gersick and Kram's in-depth interviews with these women at midlife include:

1. Whereas for men, separateness seems to be an indicator of maturity, for women, relationships are of fundamental importance to the construction of their lives. (This supports Gilligan's findings on female emotional and moral development.)
2. Women saw a difference between leadership and being at the top. In a male hierarchy, being at the top means being dominant. For these women, the role of the leader was to be a catalyst. In their view, an adaptive organization was one with multiple leaders serving as catalysts.
3. Most women interviewed wanted promotions and other rewards for their contributions at work, but were not prepared to devote themselves to 'strategizing' solely for the purpose of getting ahead in the business world.

This final point is perhaps the most important. Women I have worked with often stay in their jobs because they need to 'hang on' until the kids get through college, or until their husband's pension kicks in. But for those who can, many high-level women leave the corporate world. In the words of one of my clients, 'It was just too boring – all those lunches where nothing was discussed but work; all those golf games; and the banter. You just had the feeling that these guys had single-oriented minds. I quit because I wanted more variety in my life' (Client conversation, 2005).

Implications for coaching

We live in a time when, more than ever, people need coaching help to find meaningful ways of interacting with others, of balancing needs of career, hobby, work and play. Many people must adjust to less favourable working conditions and seek to design new and meaningful lives for themselves. Many executive coaches agree that the major source of their coaching involves helping people adjust to these new realities.

1. Help your client distinguish between her own feelings and the behaviour required of her by the organization. Encourage her to be herself within practical limits.
2. Much of current work experience involves change, insecurity and upheaval. You may need to help your client deal with both the resulting emotions and the practical issues. Often, clients who have been laid off are likely to need a lot of support. Concentrate on self-esteem issues and the importance of seeing the glass half full, not half empty.
3. For many people, the work they do is a reflection of their identity, their self-esteem, and their sense of well-being. Because people bring themselves to work, as coaches we can help clients be aware of their emotions and how they play out in the work environment.
4. Consider explaining Tannen's male–female dichotomies to your client if he or she has trouble communicating with a boss, employee or partner of the opposite sex.
5. The concept of emotional labour can be a helpful insight for anyone whose work involves constant interactions with customers.

Chapter 13: Psychometrics: from IQ to Myers-Briggs and beyond

I have found that the use of *psychometric tools* in my leadership coaching practice is a powerful way of enabling clients to experience heightened awareness and insight about the professional issues they are facing which prevent them from making the transformative changes they are looking for. All leaders want to be acknowledged for the work they do, whether on a team or in a leadership position. Like my own coach first recommended to me, I recommend to my clients at the onset of the coaching relationship that they first use a personality or behavioural preference profile – such as the MBTI or DiSC etc – to uncover what their preferences are when holding a leadership, peer or subordinate position within their organization.

Personality and Behaviour Preference Profiles are eye openers because they allow the client to discover how their own preferences and the preferences of others routinely intersect, both positively and negatively, and sometimes without our knowing why. Rather than letting the client off the hook, when they say, 'Why can't they be like me?', ask the client, 'How did you feel when your ideas were not acknowledged?' or 'What could you do next time to prepare your team?' As the client comes to possess this new awareness, insights are often the end result. With the help of coaching, the client becomes comfortable at testing behaviours and goal-oriented scenarios. With practice, clients are able to harness this awareness and insight to create stronger relationships and pursue their leadership development goals, or to discover new career or vocational possibilities.

If personality and behaviour preferences are the foundation, and leadership development or skill building is the infrastructure, then Social + Emotional Intelligence Quotient (S+EQ) is the mortar that connects everything together for clients. Regardless of what school of EQ you espouse, coaching for EQ has been found to be an effective tool for clients to discover and label their feelings, emotions, gut-level instincts or reactions, and to connect these to their source, recognizing their effects on their perceptions and their body, and using these feelings as a valuable source of insight, information and action.

Howard Fox, MA
Chicago, Illinois, USA
Fox Coaching Inc
howardfox@foxcoaching.com

The tyranny of IQ

For centuries people have been weighed and assessed, most commonly according to social class or moral virtue. Non-judgemental systems for categorizing people are equally familiar. Astrology allows for 12 types, and believers claim to be able to tell a Taurus from an Aries.

Twentieth-century psychology gave a boost to both kinds of categorization – the evaluative and the value-free. One major part of this story concerns the proliferating systems for recognizing and celebrating human difference. The earlier part is about the rise of IQ as a force in education and recruitment and the alternatives that developed in response to it.

Binet and Goddard: the invention of IQ

It was Alfred Binet (1857–1911), an experimental psychologist at the Sorbonne, who first designed what we would now recognize as an intelligence test. In 1904 he was asked by the French minister of public education to find a way of identifying children who might be in need of special support. His test assigned a 'mental age' that could be compared with the child's chronological age. In 1911, a German psychologist William Stern proposed a simple calculation to reduce the findings to a single score: divide the mental age by the chronological age and multiply by a hundred. IQ as we know it today was born. As a way of categorizing children it was seductively simple, and it added to the sense that some real, innate and invariable capacity had been identified.

Binet himself had warned against equating the result of his test with intelligence itself and turning the result into a self-fulfilling prophecy. His aim was to help children who had fallen behind, not to label them. But the IQ genie was out of the bottle.

H. H. Goddard (1856–1957), the director of research at the Vineland Training School for Feeble-Minded Girls and Boys in New Jersey, latched on to the concept of IQ and promoted it enthusiastically, believing that it described an inherited mental capacity that was fixed and measurable. Goddard's principle concern was to classify more precisely those who were considered high-grade defectives. Clear markers were already established for the lowest levels of ability. In a system of labelling that sounds crude to modern ears, those unable to master speech were categorized as 'idiots'; those whose abilities fell short of written language were described as 'imbeciles'. Goddard himself had taken the Greek word *morus*, meaning 'foolish', and coined the word 'moron' to describe those significantly below average but above the 'imbecile' level. Now he had a test that would place children objectively in these various categories.

Where Binet had pushed for remedial help for the less able, Goddard argued for them to be excluded from academic education and, as adults, from the democratic process. As a eugenicist he was also concerned to discourage or prevent the mentally deficient from breeding. His research included testing immigrants from Europe newly arriving at Ellis Island. He was surprised by his findings: abysmally low scores suggested that the great majorities of Russians, Hungarians, Italians and Jews seeking admission to the United States were at the level of 'moron' or below.

If an illiterate peasant, arriving in a foreign country after weeks of arduous travel, is instructed through a translator to perform tasks that bear no relation to his life experience, you might expect him to perform badly. A variety of environmental factors, long- and short-term, are ranged against him. The startlingly poor results recorded by Goddard's researchers might have raised questions about the validity of these tests as a way of assessing the potential of schoolchildren. Children raised in poverty and deprivation, lacking intellectual stimulation, could be expected to underperform. But Goddard's faith in the reliability of the tests was not shaken. He was confident that they measured something real and innate. Though these concerns were raised, the fashion for IQ testing was about to take a firm grip on American society.

In 1916, Lewis Terman, a professor at Stanford University, extended Binet's test, renaming it the Stanford-Binet IQ test. Terman argued that all children should be tested to determine what kind of occupations they would be suited to in adult life. By the 1960s the Wechsler Adult Intelligence Scale and the Wechsler Intelligence Scale for Children, developed by the American psychologist David Wechsler, had overtaken the Stanford-Binet test in popularity, and remains the most commonly used test today.

Spearman and Burt: the power of statistics

While Binet was measuring the cognitive abilities of French school children, the British psychologist Charles Spearman (1863–1945) was approaching the question of intelligence from a more theoretical direction. In 1904, he published a paper called 'General Intelligence Objectively Measured and Defined'.

As well as being a psychologist, Spearman was a statistician. The evidence for intelligence as a real measurable quality depends on statistics, specifically on the process of comparing results to observe correlations. Spearman's great contribution to statistics was the development of factor analysis. This is the process by which statisticians measure the level of correlation between results in order to identify common factors. This subject can be daunting for the non-specialist, but it's worth understanding some of the basic principles.

Statistical correlations are commonplace, and are sometimes, but not always, meaningful. The positive correlation between smoking and lung cancer, observed in the 1950s, contributed to the discovery that smoking is carcinogenic: it turned out there was a direct causal connection. In contrast, the positive correlation between my age and the price of fish tells us nothing except that prices tend to rise over time. If, within a particular adult population, we notice a correlation between height and income, it might perhaps point to a common factor that has contributed to both, such as the level of privilege or deprivation in childhood. Perhaps poor children get less nourishment and less education, so they are destined to be shorter and earn less.

There are interesting correlations among the different kinds of task that are included in IQ tests. It seems that if you have an extensive vocabulary, you are more likely to be able to complete a sequence of abstract shapes. For the defenders of general intelligence, these correlations are important, because they seem to point to a common underlying factor. Such correlations lay at the heart of Spearman's claim to have objectively measured general intelligence. By statistical analysis, he had identified, in his view, a single common factor, which he called g.

Such correlations are not inevitable. If, for example, a sample of the population were tested on their knowledge of characters in Jane Austen's novels and on their skill at playing Grand Theft Auto, we might find a *negative* correlation, because reading nineteenth-century fiction and playing video games are activities that generally appeal to different kinds of people. Obviously, in both these tests, environmental factors – what books you've read, how many computer games you've played – are hugely important.

But how free from environmental influence are traditional IQ tests? Is it really possible to devise a test that bypasses what has been culturally acquired and gains access to an innate mental capacity? For some people, these correlations clinch the argument for general intelligence. For others, they show its circularity – IQ tests include the kinds of task that people with high IQs are good at.

These questions matter because of the uses to which IQ tests have been put. Spearman's disciple, Cyril Burt, had an unshakeable belief in g as an inherited trait, defining it as innate, general, cognitive ability. He considered that, on the basis of a single numerical value for g, children could meaning-fully be placed in rank order. Burt worked for many years as an educational psychologist for the London County Council, where his responsibilities included identifying the 'feeble-minded' children. His work was highly influ-ential in the establishment of the 11-plus system in Britain, under the 1944 Education Act, which established a nationwide system of testing children to

separate the minority who would be set on a path towards university education from the rest. The belief that future potential could be predicted at the
age of 10 was given a huge boost by Burt's work.

After his death it was alleged that Burt had falsified some of his data.
Supporters suspected that these allegations were politically motivated. But it
became clear that he had indeed fabricated research findings, exaggerating the
number of subjects in his study of separated twins and doctoring his test
results. Though humane and scholarly in much of his work, Burt's obsession
with the heritability of intelligence had led him into academic fraud. (For
more on the fascinating early history of IQ testing, see Stephen Jay Gould's
The Mismeasure of Man, 1981.)

Sternberg and Gardner: multiple intelligences

Ever since the idea of a single scientifically measurable capacity known as
'intelligence' was first proposed, it has had its opponents. In the 1930s, Louis
Thurstone (1887–1955), a psychologist at the University of Chicago, proposed
a more complicated model. His research suggested that there were seven
primary mental abilities: verbal comprehension, word fluency, number facility,
spatial visualization, associative memory, perceptual speed and reasoning.

In the 1980s, two prominent American psychologists were working
independently on the problem. Robert Sternberg (1949–) proposed a triarchic
theory of intelligence (Sternberg 1985), dividing mental ability into three
kinds: analytical, creative and practical.

Sternberg argued that intelligence is contextual. Any assessment of
it must vary according to social or cultural context, and what constitutes
an intelligent act may differ from one person to another. This is not the same
as saying that it doesn't have an objective existence as a function of the
brain, but it does mean that how people express their intelligence will vary
according to context. This has interesting implications for intelligence tests,
suggesting that they would need to be far more culturally specific than the
established ones.

In *Frames of Mind* (1983), Howard Gardner (1943–), a Harvard psychologist,
broadened the concept of intelligence further, proposing seven types: linguistic,
logical-mathematical, spatial, bodily-kinaesthetic, musical, interpersonal and
intrapersonal. He pointed out that conventional academic education largely
consists of the first two and tends to neglect or undervalue the rest. This
deconstruction of the concept of intelligence is considerably more radical than
Thurstone's, whose list is heavily weighted towards the linguistic, logical and
mathematical abilities that constitute only two of Gardner's seven types.

In the preface to the second edition of his book, Gardner expressed
surprise at how controversial his theory had turned out to be: he had not been
aware of 'the extent to which these conceptions of intelligence and intelligence
testing are entrenched in our society' (Gardner 1985: ix). He acknowledges the

positive correlations among different IQ-related abilities – the tendency for someone who scores well in one area to also score well in another – but rejects this as proof of a single overarching capacity called 'intelligence', arguing that the abilities that are measured in IQ tests are less varied than they might appear: 'Nearly all current tests are so devised that they call principally upon linguistic and logical facilities (as well as a certain speed, flexibility, and perhaps superficiality as well).' For Gardner, an assessment of spatial intelligence – to take one example – should not be based on one more paper and pencil test requiring multiple choice responses, but should involve navigation about an unfamiliar environment.

The continuing appeal of the IQ test

Nevertheless, many psychologists remain convinced of the existence of 'general intelligence' as a measurable capacity. Ian Deary, a professor of pyschology at the University of Edinburgh is in favour of IQ testing, citing evidence that an IQ test is one of the most useful predictors of how well an employee will perform in a job, equal in effectiveness to the more time-consuming 'structured interview', and much better than common selection methods such as unstructured interviews and reference checks (Deary 2001: 95–7). For this reason, various forms of IQ testing still feature in the interviewing process for some jobs in the business world.

Deary rejects Gardner's theory of multiple intelligences, asserting that intelligence as traditionally measured and understood is distinct from, and more important than, other kinds of talent. But in defending the supremacy of IQ in the face of Gardner's more varied range of attributes, he comes up with a revealing list of what IQ testing leaves out:

> [T]ests of mental abilities . . . do not measure creativity or wisdom. Neither of these is easy to measure, though both have some demonstrable associations with intelligence. Mental ability tests do not measure personality, social adroitness, leadership, charisma, cool-headedness, altruism, or many other things that we value. But that proper point is not the same as saying that they are useless. (Deary 2001: 16)

IQ testing has taken a long journey from being the means to put children in rank order according to their future potential, to being one tool among many for selecting candidates for a job.

The bell curve controversy

And yet the potential remains for arguments over IQ to be politically explosive. When a Harvard psychologist, Richard J. Herrnstein, and a political scientist, Charles Murray, argued in *The Bell Curve* (1994) that there are large differences in average IQ between racial groups in the USA, and that genetics play a significant part in these differences, they created a storm of controversy.

They report that, whereas the bell curve for white Americans is centred just above 100, for American Jews and East Asians it is higher, for Latinos lower, and for African Americans lower still, on 85. They acknowledge that there is no settled view within the scientific community as to what causes these differences and admit that they 'considered leaving the genetics issue at that, on grounds that no useful purpose is served by talking about a subject that is so inflammatory, so painful, and so far from resolution' (Hernstein and Murray 1994: 296). But they talk about it anyway, at considerable length, concluding that these gaps show no sign of diminishing; that IQ is the most important determinant of economic success in life; and that social policy directed towards raising the performance of African Americans to the level of white Americans is misguided. If there is a way of thinking outside the IQ box, this book doesn't manage it.

The authors claim a high level of scientific rigour; but how rigorous can any of this be? They acknowledge that they have no objective definition of membership in one racial group or another, but depend on 'self-classification'. Is the rest of it any more objective? How effectively can genetic factors be disentangled from environmental ones? Neuroscience is unlikely to locate intelligence any time soon. Meanwhile, we rely on something fuzzier. Who defines which qualities or talents fall within our definition of intelligence? Who determines what constitutes success at school, or at work? Who judges whether any of this is, or is not, culturally biased?

A century after Goddard was testing the IQs of newly arrived immigrants at Ellis Island it is easy to spot the extent to which his self-proclaimed objectivity was distorted by cultural assumptions. How confident can the authors and supporters of the *Bell Curve* be that they are not stuck in their own labyrinth of circular arguments?

Considering the current state of our economies, and the misjudgements that brought us here, we might ask ourselves whether the systems we've devised for identifying, developing and rewarding human talent are as good as they might be.

Daniel Goleman and Meredith Belbin: the limits of IQ

There is growing evidence that intelligence as traditionally understood has been overrated. In the mid-90s, the psychologist and science journalist Daniel Goleman (1946–) put emotional intelligence on the map with his bestselling book of that name, followed a decade later by *Social Intelligence: The new science of human relationships*. Goleman defines four areas of emotional intelligence: self-awareness, self-management, social awareness and relationship management (Goleman 1996). This new vision of intelligence chimes with a commonly recognized truth: that as social creatures, our ability to communicate effectively and engage constructively with each other is at least as important as what we are capable of doing alone inside our own heads.

What's more, success at work is dependent not only on rounded individuals but on rounded teams. The most effective teams are not created simply by putting the brightest people together, *whatever* measure of brightness is being used.

Research by Meredith R. Belbin (1926–) (*Management Teams*, 1981) involved constructing 'companies' that would compete in a business simulation game called 'Teamopoly'. In the early stages Belbin and his fellow researchers took the think-tank approach and put all the clever people in the same room, calling them the Apollo team. The assumption of the other participants, who were quick to spot the criteria for Apollo membership, was that this was unfair: the Apollos were bound to win. Not so, as it turned out. The first Apollo team came last. Over time, the record of Apollo teams was consistently dismal. This counter-intuitive discovery gave a boost to Belbin's research, leaving an open question: What combination of team members is most likely to lead to success?

He came up with eight useful people to have in teams: the Company Worker, the Chairman, the Shaper, the Plant, the Resource Investigator, the Monitor-Evaluator, the Team Worker and the Completer-Finisher. Each brings different qualities to the team. Each kind has different strengths and weaknesses, but in combination they can achieve more than a line-up of individual winners.

The celebration of difference

It is interesting to consider what Carl Jung would have made of the dispute between those who are attracted to the idea of intelligence as a numerically measurable entity, and those who instinctively mistrust it. Such disputes form a substantial part of his book *Psychological Types*, published in 1920. In fact, the book seems to spring partly from an attempt to understand the source of such disagreements in his own life, touching on one disagreement in particular.

Carl Jung and the roots of conflict

By the time he was developing his theory of types, Jung had already parted company with Sigmund Freud. Another of Freud's earliest and closest associates, Alfred Adler, had also broken away to form his own school of psychotherapy. In *Psychological Types*, Jung contrasts the approaches of Freud and Adler, identifying Freud's as essentially extraverted because, being rooted in repressed sexual wishes, it is about the individual in relation to the external desired object. On the other hand, Adler's interest in the development of a strong ego is essentially introverted. In Jung's view, this difference lies at the heart of their failure to agree (Jung 1991: 61–2). Jung, like Adler an introvert, sees his own split with Freud in similar terms:

> For everyone whose guiding principle is adaptation to external reality, imagination is for these reasons reprehensible and useless. And yet we know that every good idea and all creative work are the offspring of the imagination, and have their source in what one is pleased to call infantile fantasy. (Jung 1991: 63)

Jung reviews a series of other disagreements and temperamental contrasts throughout history and finds this archetypal conflict between the introvert and the extrovert repeatedly played out. For Jung, these two attitudes, as he calls them, are a crucial cause of division among people.

Separate from this, he argues, we are all equipped with four functions: sensation, thinking, feeling and intuition.

> The essential function of sensation is to establish that something exists, thinking tells us what it means, feeling what its value is, and intuition surmises whence it comes and whither it goes. Sensation and intuition I call irrational functions, because they are both concerned simply with what happens and with actual or potential realities. Thinking and feeling, being discriminative functions, are rational. (Jung 1983: 144)

It may seem odd that *feeling* is put alongside *thinking* as a 'rational' function. The point is that they are alternative ways of assessing the significance of something in the light of experience. A *feeling* response is concerned with whether it is good or bad, pleasant or unpleasant. Just as our way of registering an event will focus either on what we learn about it from our five senses or on what our sixth sense tells us about it, but not both, so we will respond to it either by reflecting on it or by evaluating it through feeling.

Combining the two attitudes with the four functions gives eight personality types. In addition, Jung says, we each have an auxiliary function from the other group. So a *thinking* type might have either sensation or intuition as an auxiliary. The other functions will be submerged in the unconscious. *Feeling* for the *thinking* type will be submerged more deeply, and therefore likely, in Jung's terms, to show up in the shadow – likely, in other words, to trip you up when you're not expecting it.

Jung is insistent that his purpose is not to reduce the complexity of human nature. People don't exhibit one attitude to the exclusion of another, or depend entirely on one function. We all draw to some extent on a range of responses. In fact, the analysis of different types grows out of his awareness of diversity:

> When one begins as a young doctor, one's head is still full of clinical pictures and diagnoses. In the course of the years, impressions of another kind accumulate. One is struck by the enormous diversity of human individuals, by the chaotic profusion of human individual cases, the special circumstances of whose lives and whose special characters produced clinical pictures that, even supposing one still felt any desire to do so, can be squeezed into the straitjacket of a diagnosis only by force. (Jung 1983: 139)

Briggs, Myers and working women

Katherine Cook Briggs (1875–1968) and her daughter Isabel Briggs Myers (1897–1980) became interested in Jung's work on psychological types during the late 1920s, but it was not until the start of the Second World War that they began to create a personality test that would become the Myers-Briggs Type Indicator (MBTI). With large numbers of men joining the forces, there was a new demand for female workers in industry. Myers and Briggs felt that women entering unfamiliar areas of employment would benefit from a psychological test to indicate what kind of work might suit them.

As Isabel Myers' son relates (in his 1995 preface to Myers' book *Gifts Differing*), when they produced the first version of the test in 1943 'they came face to face with a double-barrelled opposition from the academic community' (Myers and Myers 1980: xiii). First, Jung's theory was not taken seriously by mainstream psychologists. Second, Myers and Briggs were considered totally unqualified, being neither psychologists nor statisticians. But they had done their homework. Though she had no formal academic training in the required disciplines, Isabel Myers had, 'for more than a year, apprenticed herself to someone who *was* a qualified expert . . . and from him she learned what she needed to know about test construction, scoring, validation, and statistics' (Myers and Myers 1980: xiii).

In the teeth of indifference and hostility from the profession, Myers continued to refine the test, encouraged by the positive response she received from people who took it and, with pleasure and relief, recognized themselves in the results.

MBTI takes Jung's two pairs of functions and pictures them as polarities: one scale running from *thinking* (T) to *feeling* (F); another from *sensing* (S) to *intuiting* (N). The two attitudes, *introverted* and *extraverted*, which have a special status in Jung's scheme, are turned into an equivalent polarity (I or E). Jung writes about sensing and intuiting as ways of *perceiving* an experience, and thinking and feeling as ways of *judging* it, and MBTI creates an additional fourth scale out of this pair of opposites (J or P). In terms of picturing and recording the different types, the Myers-Briggs model is simpler than Jung's, without any loss in terms of analytical subtlety. Someone who would have been described by Jung as 'an extraverted intuiting type with an auxiliary thinking function' becomes, in the language of Myers-Briggs, an ENTJ or an ENTP.

From its obscure beginnings, MBTI has become one of the most familiar and universally recognized psychometric tests. What accounts for its huge success? To begin with, it has face validity: people tend to recognize the truthfulness of what it tells them about themselves. It also fulfils more stringent criteria: for example, it can be repeated with consistent results. In practical terms, it offers a useful and satisfying degree of complexity combined with the simplicity of a model that can be easily grasped and pictured.

Any method that helps the individual understand the ways in which he is different from other people, and that does so without introducing unnecessary value judgements, is likely to be helpful and reassuring. Anything that validates one's particular way of responding to things without devaluing the alternative ways will encourage self-acceptance and tolerance of others. If the individual recognizes himself and others in the results he is enlightened about one of the most perplexing frustrations of human interaction: why others don't see or think or behave the same way he does.

Some people are resistant to being categorized; some are ideologically opposed to any system that blurs the uniqueness of the individual. But more often people respond with recognition and gratitude to a test that allows them to be valued for who they are. Some level of categorizing, as long as it coincides with our own experience, is comforting: we are neither all alike, nor all alone.

The popularity of MBTI has led some to think of it as an elaborate parlour game. There are many who know their Myers-Briggs type without having explored its significance in any depth. It is easy to emphasize the positive aspects of every preference and forget its Jungian shadow. As with any psychometric instrument, the result is only as useful as the conversation it leads to.

Wonder Woman and normal people

In the early 1940s, while Katherine Cook Briggs and Isabel Briggs Myers were developing MBTI in order to help women entering employment, William Moulton Marston (1893–1947), a psychologist who had earned his doctorate at Harvard, was busy creating a new feminine role model: the comic book heroine Wonder Woman.

In the age of Superman, Marston was conscious of the impact comic book archetypes could have on children and wanted to encourage female empowerment and a more feminine notion of strength. In inventing the character of Wonder Woman (under the pseudonym Charles Moulton and in partnership with H. G. Peter), he drew inspiration from two powerful women – his wife, Elizabeth Holloway Marston, and the woman who shared their home and their life, Olive Byrne. A superhero, engaged in the early years in fighting Nazis, Wonder Woman has been described as a 'distinctly feminist role model whose mission was to bring the Amazon ideals of love, peace, and sexual equality to a world torn by the hatred of men' (Philip Charles Crawford, 'The Legacy of Wonder Woman', *School Library Journal,* 1 March 2007).

In his capacity as a professional psychologist Marston was already well known for his book, *Emotions of Normal People*, containing his DISC theory of human behaviour. Like Wonder Woman, that book can be seen as an attempt to promote a gentler, more harmonious vision:

> I do not regard you as a 'normal person', emotionally, when you are suffering from fear, rage, pain, shock, desire to deceive, or any emotional state whatsoever containing turmoil and conflict. Your emotional responses are 'normal' when they produce pleasantness and harmony. (Moulton 1928: 1–2)

In Marston's view, research into how people function tended to focus on moments of *dys*function, such as the fight or flight response. As a result, violent emotions come to be seen as an inevitable and even necessary element of human interaction:

> If a jungle beast is torn and wounded during the course of an ultimately victorious battle, it would be a spurious logic indeed that attributed its victory to its wounds. If a human being be emotionally torn and mentally disorganized by fear or rage during a business battle from which, ultimately, he emerges victorious, it seems equally nonsensical to ascribe his conquering strength to those emotions symptomatic of his temporary weakness and defeat. (Moulton 1928: 2)

The DISC theory focuses instead on 'normal' emotional states. According to Marston, I experience my environment as either favourable or antagonistic, and my response is either passive or active. Presenting these as two axes at right angles to each other, Marston constructs a grid of four quadrants. Each quadrant represents one of four kinds of behaviour: Dominance, Inducement, Submission and Compliance. In an antagonistic environment, dominance produces activity, and compliance produces passivity. In a favourable environment, inducement produces activity, and submission produces passivity. All of these are valid responses, and all of them can lead to harmonious outcomes.

Marston's theory has given rise to two different assessments: DISC, which measures dominance, influence, steadiness and compliance; and DiSC (with a lowercase *i*) where the fourth behaviour is called *conscientiousness*. Both can be used with an individual or a team to foster awareness, enhance individual or team performance, develop better communication, and reduce conflict.

The authors of these assessments, while adopting Marston's framework, found it necessary to change either two or three of his key terms, finding more positive-sounding replacements for words that are perhaps suggestive of traditionally feminine wiles and weaknesses. Interestingly, Marston himself, a man comfortable in the company of dominant women and the inventor of the first comic book super-heroine, saw 'submission' as an equally serviceable preference, irrespective of gender.

Will Schutz on wanting and expressing

A very different approach to understanding how people function in teams originated in work conducted in the US Navy in the mid-50s. Will Schutz, a psychologist on active duty, was asked to find how teams working aboard ships could be helped to cooperate more effectively. His findings were first published in book form in *FIRO: A Three-Dimensional Theory of Interpersonal Behavior* (1958).

What Schutz observed was that, just as we need food and shelter, so we have interpersonal needs that affect our interactions with others. If our particular needs are not met, we can become uncomfortable or anxious. But the extent of these needs can vary considerably from one person to another. He encapsulated this in his theory of Fundamental Interpersonal Relations Orientation (FIRO), in which he proposed that the way we relate to each other reveals three dimensions of need: inclusion, control and affection. He created an instrument for measuring behaviour along these three dimensions, which he called FIRO-B, where B stands for behaviour.

Each need comes in two forms: what you *express* to others – the extent to which you initiate that behaviour; and what you *want* from others – the extent to which you desire or will accept that behaviour. In one-to-one relationships, how much affection do you express, and to what extent do you want others to show affection towards you? In group settings, how inclined are you to include others, and how much do you want to be included? In decision making, how important is it for you to take control or exert influence, and how much will you accept direction and want others to take the lead?

More recently, Schutz described the development of FIRO-B as 'the climax of what I've come to see as my first scientific phase' (Schutz 1994: 3). During the 1960s he began to experience a range of experimental techniques, including psychodrama, gestalt therapy and Rolfing. He conducted T-groups for the National Training Laboratories in Bethen, Maine and encounter groups at the Esalen Institute (Chapter 2). In his work with organizations he became increasingly interested in the way groups functioned and 'more and more attracted to the idea of self-concept as the key to solving organizational problems, and to universal self-esteem as the goal for the organization'. He found himself confronted with the 'human element' as a stumbling block – the 'personal fears, rigidities, defences, and all the other real reasons why human events do not take place more smoothly in organizations' (Schutz 1994: 10). He came to see that 'resistance to change is much greater than I had imagined' (Schutz 1994: 249).

These experiences led him to eight key insights:

1. the importance of truth in all our relationships
2. the extent to which we choose our own lives
3. the profound importance of simplicity
4. the limitlessness of human potential
5. the holistic interrelation among thoughts, behaviour, feelings and the body
6. the importance of completing unfinished experience
7. the basic dimensions of human functioning are inclusion, control and openness
8. self-esteem lies at the root of all behaviour. (Schutz 1994: 210)

A FIRO-B assessment is not always a comfortable experience. Whoever I am, I can wear my Myers-Briggs type as a badge of honour; every location on the DiSC map has its attractions; my FIRO-B results might be more problematical. Whereas MTBI and DiSC celebrate human difference, FIRO-B touches on the personal baggage we bring into our dealings with each other. It focuses on our behaviour rather than how we process experience, and is rooted in an understanding of the ways in which our behaviour has been shaped by our earliest relationships. We tend to repeat the roles we either practised as children or observed in the behaviour of our parents. If I was smothered with love as a child, I might want or express too much affection in adult life. If I was given too little guidance, I might grow up unwilling to take responsibility.

Schutz's model straddles a crucial paradox: every way of being is valid, but some behaviours make for more productive relationships. What holds this paradox together is self-esteem, the single most important factor lying at the heart of any relationship. Schutz recognizes the damage people can suffer in childhood and how debilitating such damage can be, but believes that human potential is without limit. We may not be able to override preferences acquired in infancy, but we can choose how to behave, how to interact, and how to function more successfully.

A plethora of instruments

MBTI, DiSC and FIRO-B, popular as they are, represent only a fraction of the instruments currently available. For coaches, the proliferation of psychometrics can be overwhelming. Instruments related to emotional intelligence include the *Emotional Competence Inventory* (ECI) and the *Emotional and Social Competency Inventory* (ESCI), both based on Daniel Goleman's work. The *Emotional Quotient Inventory* (EQ-i), developed by Reuven Bar-On, is a self-report measure of emotional and social intelligence that identifies 15 factors, such as impulse control, flexibility, empathy and assertiveness.

Other instruments take a range of approaches to the question of what makes us tick. The *Birkman Method* explores interpersonal style, underlying motivation, expectations and response to stress. Edgar Schein's *Career Anchors* self-assessment identifies eight motivators. Which of these motivators drives you – a preference for autonomy, entrepreneurial creativity or service to a cause, for example – will determine what kind of career you will find satisfying.

Marcus Buckingham and Donald Clifton argue that developing strengths is a more effective strategy than working on weaknesses. Their *Clifton StrengthFinder* aims to identify your five signature themes out of a list of 34. The *Values in Action* (VIA) survey of character strengths, developed by Martin Seligman and Christopher Peterson, measures 24 possible strengths, such as creativity, curiosity and open-mindedness. The Learning Styles Inventory (LSI) is based on the David Kolb's experiential learning theory and is designed to identify your favoured learning style.

There are a number of instruments based on Costa and McRae's Five Factor Model, such as their own *NEO Five-Factor Inventory* (NEO-FFI) and *NEO Personality Inventory-Revised* (NEO-PI-R). The *Hogan Personality Inventory* (HPI) applies the Five-Factor Model more directly to the world of business, distinguishing between 'primary scales' such as sensitivity, prudence and inquisitiveness, and 'occupational scales' such as reliability and sales potential.

Instruments focusing on leadership qualities include *Leadership Effectiveness Analysis* (LEA), which provides feedback on 22 separate competencies, and the *Leadership Practices Inventory* (LPI 360), developed by James Kouzes and Barry Posner as a way of scoring a range of behaviours on a 10-point scale.

In addition to the *Belbin Team Role Questionnaire*, instruments focusing on how people work together include the *Team Development Assessment*, which was developed by Charles Pellerin, a former director of NASA's astrophysics division, and the Parker Team Player Survey (TPS), which identifies four team member styles: contributor, collaborator, communicator and challenger. The *Thomas Kilmann Conflict Model Instrument* looks specifically at how people deal with conflict: by competing, collaborating, compromising, avoiding or accommodating.

This list, which is far from complete, gives an indication of the sheer diversity of psychometric instruments available to coaches. If there was ever a time when a single numerical score seemed enough to identify someone's potential, that time is long past. Even so, the danger remains of being mesmerized by the result of this or that measurement. To inform my client that he's an ISTJ Monitor Evaluator with Steadiness as his primary style might be as much use as telling him he's a Capricorn, unless I know how to develop that insight in a coaching conversation. As with any coaching tool, the effectiveness of a psychometric test lies in the capacity of the coach to help the client both understand his thinking and behaviour and, if necessary, to modify both. Psychometrics work when the client and the coach between them turn them to good use.

Implications for coaching

1. It has become increasingly important to understand the concept of emotional intelligence. Encouraging your client to become more attuned to her own and other people's emotions can be immensely valuable.
2. Skillful coaches often use one or more assessments or psychometric tests when working with a client. It is useful to have a range of instruments at your disposal, to have a sense of which might be appropriate at any particular stage, and to give time to exploring the results in a way that is enlightening for the client.
3. Some psychometric exercises can be useful in identifying not just the client's strengths, but also in what areas she uses those strengths (see, for example, the Approaches to Happiness exercise on Seligman's Authentic Happiness website).
4. It is important for us to be aware of our own types, strengths and preferences when working with a client. The client may think or feel in ways that are unfamiliar to us.
5. As clever as many of these instruments are in measuring abilities and identifying challenges, the instrument is only as good as the coaching conversation that follows it.

Bibliography

Anderson, W. T. (2004) *The Upstart Spring: Esalen and the human potential movement: The first twenty years*. Lincoln, Nebraska: iUniverse.

Bandler, R. and Grinder, J. (1979) *Frogs into Princes: Neuro-linguistic programming*. London: Eden Grove Press.

Bartley, W. W. III (1978) *Werner Erhard: The transformation of a man: The founding of est*. New York: Clarkson N. Potter.

Beck, A. T. (1976) *Cognitive Therapy and the Emotional Disorders*. New York: Penguin Group.

Berne, E. (1968) *Games People Play*. London: Penguin Group.

Berne, E. (2010) *A Montreal Childhood*. Seville, Spain: Jeder.

Bion, W. R. (1961) *Experiences in Groups*. New York: Routledge.

Belbin, R. M. (1981) *Management Teams: Why they succeed or fail*. Oxford: Butterworth Heinemann.

Brown, J. A. C. (1987) *Freud and the Post-Freudians*. Harmondsworth: Penguin Books.

Burns, D. (1980) *Feeling Good: The new mood therapy*. New York: Avon Books.

Burns, D. (1999) *The Feeling Good Handbook*. New York: The Penguin Group.

Butler-Bowdon, T. (2007) *50 Psychology Classics*. London: Nicholas Brealey Publishing.

Capra, F. *Homage to Gregory Bateson*. An Ecology of Mind website: http://www.anecologyofmind.com/reviews/

Carnegie, D. (1998) *How to Win Friends and Influence People*. London: Ebury Press.

Crews, F. C. (ed.) (1998) *Unauthorized Freud: Doubters confront a legend*. New York: Viking Penguin.

Deary, J. J. (2001) *Intelligence: A very short introduction*. Oxford: Oxford University Press.

Eliot, T. S. (1964) *T. S. Eliot Selected Poems*. New York: Harcourt Brace Jovanovich.

Erdman, D. V. (ed.) (1988) *The Complete Poetry and Prose of William Blake*. New York: Doubleday.

Fordham, F. (1964) *An Introduction to Jung's Psychology*, Harmondsworth: Penguin Books.

Frankl, V. (2004) *Man's Search For Meaning*. London: Rider.

Gallwey, T. W. (1986) *The Inner Game of Tennis*. London: Pan Macmillan.

Gallwey, T. W. (2009) *The Inner Game of Stress: Outsmart life's challenges and fulfill your potential*. New York: Random House.

Gardner, H. (1985) *Frames of Mind: The theory of multiple intelligences*. New York: HarperCollins.

Gersick, G. and Kram, K. (2002) High Achieving Women at Midlife: An exploratory study, *Journal of Management Inquiry*, 11(2).

Ginsberg, A. (1961) *Howl, Kaddish and Other Poems*. London: Penguin Group.

Goleman, D. (1996) *Emotional Intelligence: Why it can matter more than IQ*. London: Bloomsbury Publishing.

Goleman, D. (2007) *Social Intelligence: The new science of human relationships*. New York: Arrow Books.

Gould, S. J. (1981) *The Mismeasure of Man*. New York: W. W. Norton.

Harris, T. (1969) *I'm OK – You're OK*. New York: HarperCollins.

Hayes, P. (2008) *NLP Coaching*. Maidenhead: Open University Press.

Henle, M. (1986) *All That, Essays in the Theory and History of Psychology*. New York: Columbia Press.

Hernstein, R. and Murray, C. (1994) *The Bell Curve: Intelligence and class structure in American life*. New York: Free Press.

Hill, C. (1975) *The World Turned Upside Down: Radical ideas during the English Revolution*. London: Penguin Books.

Hill, N. (2009) *Think and Grow Rich*. West Sussex: Capstone Publishing.

Hillman, J. and Ventura, M. (1992) *We've had a Hundred Years of Psychotherapy and the World's getting Worse*. New York: HarperCollins.

Hochschild, A. (2005) *The Managed Heart: Commercialization of human feeling*. Berkeley: University of California Press.

Hoffman, L. (1981) *Foundations of Family Therapy*. New York: Basic Books.

Huxley, A. (2009) *The Doors of Perception: Heaven and Hell*. New York: HarperCollins.

James. W. (1982) *The Varieties of Religious Experience*. New York: The Penguin American Library.

Jung, C. G. (1933) *Modern Man in Search of a Soul*. Orlando, Florida: Harcourt Brace Jovanovich.

Jung, C. G. (1965) *Memories, Dreams, Reflections*. New York: Vintage Books.

Jung, C. G. (1983) *The Essential Jung*. London: Fontana Press.

Jung, C. G. (1991) *Psychological Types*. London: Routledge.

Kerr, M. E. and Bowen, M. (1988) *Family Evaluation. An approach based on Bowen Theory*. New York: Basic Books.

Kirschenbaum, H. and Henderson, V. L. (eds) (1989) *The Carl Rogers Reader*. New York: Houghton Mifflin Company.

Lasch, C. (1979) *The Culture of Narcissism: American Life in An Age of Diminishing Expectations*. New York: W. W. Norton.

Leonard, G. and Murphy, M. (1995) *The Life We Are Given: A long-term program for realizing the potential of body, mind, heart, and soul*. New York: A Jeremy Tarcher/ Putnam Book.

Lewin, K. (1997) *Resolving Social Conflicts and Field Theory in Social Science*. Illustrated reprint: American Psychological Association.

Litwin, A. (2011) Women Working Together: Understanding Women's Relations at Work. *CGO Insights*, Center for Gender and Organizations Briefing Note Number 33, March 2011.

Lowen, A. (1958) *The Language of the Body*. New York: Macmillan Publishing.

Maslow, A. H. (1968) *Toward a Psychology of Being*. New York: Van Nostrand Reinhold.

Milgram, S. (1969) *Obedience to Authority: An experimental view*. New York: Harper and Row.

Mills, C. W. (1959) *The Sociological Imagination*. Oxford: Oxford University Press.

Minuchin, S. (1993) *Family Healing: Strategies for hope and understanding*. New York: Touchstone.

Moulton, M. W. (1928) *Emotions of Normal People*. London: Kegan Paul.

Myers, I. B. and Myers, P. B. (1980) *Gifts Differing: Understanding personality type*. Palo Alto, California: Davies-Black Publishing.

Nichols, M. P. and Schwartz, R. C. (1995) *Family Therapy: Concepts and Methods*, 3rd edition. Massachusetts: Simon and Schuster.

Pearson, C. (1991) *Awakening the Heroes Within*. New York: HarperCollins.

Peltier, B. (2010) *The Psychology of Executive Coaching: Theory and application*. New York: Routledge.

Prochaska, J. O. et al. (1992) In Search of How People Change. *American Psychologist*, September 1992: 1102.

Ram Dass (1970) *The Only Dance There Is*. New York: Anchor Books.

Ram Dass (1987) *Grist for the Mill*. Berkeley, California: Celestial Arts.

Ram Dass (2000) *Still Here*. New York: Penguin Putnam.

Reich, W. (1993) *The Function of the Orgasm: Sex-economic problems of biological energy*. Channel Islands, UK: The Guernsey Press.

Robertson, N. (1988) *Getting Better: Inside Alcoholics Anonymous*. New York: William Morrow and Company.

Rogers, C. R. (1961) *On Becoming a Person: A therapist's view of psychotherapy*. New York: Houghton Mifflin.

Rowan, J. (1976) *Ordinary Ecstasy: The dialectics of humanistic psychology*. East Sussex: Routledge.

Rowan, J. (1993) *The Transpersonal: Spirituality in psychotherapy and counselling*. London: Routledge.

Sale, K. (1995) *Rebels Against the Future: The Luddites and their war on the Industrial Revolution*. Reading, Massachusetts: Addison-Wesley Publishing.

Schultz, S. (1984) *Family Systems Thinking*. New Jersey: Jason Aronson.

Schutz, W. C. (1967) *Joy: Expanding Human Awareness*. New York: Grove Press.

Schutz, W. C. (1971) *Here Comes Everybody: Bodymind and encounter culture*. New York: Harper and Row Publishers.

Schutz, W. C. (1994) *The Human Element: Productivity, self-esteem, and the bottom line*. San Francisco: Jossey-Bass.

Seiler, A. (2003) *Coaching to the Human Soul: Ontological coaching and deep change*, volume 1: *The Linguistic Basis of Ontological Coaching*. Victoria: Newfield, Australia.

Sennett, R. (1998) *The Corrosion of Character: The personal consequences of work in the new capitalism*. New York: W. W. Norton.

Sharaf, M. (1994) *Fury on Earth: A biography of Wilhelm Reich*. Cambridge, Massachusetts: Da Capo Press.

Sternberg, R. J. (1985) *Beyond IQ: A triarchic theory of human intelligence*. Cambridge: Cambridge University Press.

Stevens, A. (1994) *Jung: A very short introduction*. Oxford: Oxford University Press.

Storr, A. (1989) *Freud: A very short introduction*. Oxford: Oxford University Press.

Tannen, D. (1994) *Talking from 9 to 5: Women and Men in the Workplace: Language, sex and power*. New York: Avon Books.

Terkel, S. (2004) *Working: People talk about what they do all day and how they feel about what they do*. New York: The New Press.

Watts, A. (1972) *In My Own Way: An autobiography 1915–1965*. Novato, California: New World Library.

Whitmore, D. (2004) *Psychosynthesis Counselling in Action*. London: Sage Publications.

Whitmore, J. (2004) *Coaching for Performance: GROWing people, performance, and purpose*. London: Nicholas Brealey Publishing.

Wood, L. S. (2010) *A More Perfect Union: Holistic worldviews and the transformation of American culture after World War II*. New York: Oxford University Press.

Index

Locators shown in *italics* refer to book titles.